MW01232534

Living the Simple Life

Written by

Martin White

PublishAmerica
Baltimore

First printing

ISBN: 1-4241-0167-0
PUBLISHED BY PUBLISHAMERICA, LLLP
www.publishamerica.com
Baltimore

Printed in the United States of America

Dedicated to:

Randy Shores,
my cousin who got lost
in today's world.

My wife, Marilyn,
for teaching me every day what
love and friendship really are.

Chapter 1
Living the Simple Life

My name is Martin White. I am a middle-aged father of three boys. I own my own computer consulting company called Micro Connections. I am writing this book to document some of the things I have learned in life and in backyard counseling. As long as I can remember people have been coming to me to talk about their problems.

I am a good listener and have an insightful way at looking at things. I call myself a backyard psychologist; this is because I have been working out people's problems, talking them through hard times. I have even saved a life; I talked a girl out of slitting her wrist, knife in hand. A lot of people have a hard time figuring out life and how to handle people and situations. I really don't feel I am smarter than anyone else. I just have a lot of experience in different people and problems.

In this book I will show you how to enjoy life and accept it for what it is. Most people I know do not enjoy life; they complain about anything and everything and are really not happy at all. I will say this many, many times in the course of this book. You and only you decide whether you are happy in life or not. What I mean is all of us have many, many kinds of problems in our lives. Each one of us decides whether this problem is going to affect our attitudes. There are only 2 things in life: the external and the internal.

What I will be talking about in this book is how to manage your internal self to make you a happier person. Happiness is not as hard as you think to achieve; it is as simple as just making up your mind that you are happy and you will be. The process is simple, but not easy. You have many years of programming that will stand in your way. You must completely believe that life is great before you will see it because there are too many negatives out there that will pull you the other way. Remember, your mind is the most powerful tool you have to break the trend, but it is like the captain of your ship; if you think positively and talk positively you will be positive. If you think negatively and talk negatively, guess what you will be? A successful person is one that eats, drinks, walks, talks, looks, breathes and thinks successfully.

It doesn't matter how much or little money you make. You might say, well if I had lots of money I would be happy. That is not true; yes, you could buy more material things, but material things are not happiness. Most of the rich people I know are totally miserable people to be around. They spend so much of their lives accumulating this fortune they have no time for themselves. Even when they get to the point of being comfortably well off, they will push themselves even harder to accumulate more, at the cost of time with their family and friends.

Happiness is not something you can buy. Happiness is something you are. Whether you are a millionaire or on skid row, you can think positive or negative thoughts. Here is an example: A millionaire finds an old couch on the side of the road near a garbage can. His negative thought is "OOOOH, that is sick." A homeless person finds the same couch and is glad to have something to sleep on. The couch didn't change, just the thoughts of the people viewing it. Am I saying that the rich guy should have taken the couch? No, it is just to point out that a material item is of no real value, that one man's trash is another man's treasure.

All of us are guilty of not appreciating what we have. I drive a nice car, what is on my mind? I wish I could have a better one. I live in a nice apartment, but I want a bigger one. I have computer equipment and I am unhappy that my computer equipment is not as nice as someone else's. This is human to have these feelings. What you can do about it is to realize it and then look around at what you have. Remember, no matter how bad you think you have it, there are thousands out there whose goals are to make it to where you have already achieved. In just focusing on the "I don't have," you will never be able to be happy.

Enjoy what you have worked so hard for. It is American to want the best, newest products and material things. It is part of the American Dream. It is OK to want those things and set goals to work for them. Don't give up the dreams, just appreciate the reality. Reality is what you already have achieved. Life is a wonderful thing, to get up and be with the ones you love and that return your love. We don't all have this, partially because of external energy (the other people around you, but mostly because of your internal energy); things like love and happiness will reflect back in many different ways when you take the time to give the energy out. It may not be a direct reflect but it will come. I have an aunt that always said, "Kill 'em with kindness." That is to be nice to them even if they are being rude to you. You will break through the negative they are putting out and they will switch to the positive you are putting off. Remember, it is no fun for a person that is pissed off to come across someone that will not react. They are looking for the person that will go with them down that negative road. Negative supports negative, and positive supports positive. Try to be positive about dealing with negative people, and you will be able to pull out the positive from the negative. I will get into this later in the book. Well, a little more about me. During my childhood, I noticed at an early age that I was outgoing. We used to do a lot of camping. Every time we went to a campground I always took it upon myself to organize all the kids that were camping that weekend and plan games, hikes, and campfires with them.

I was never bashful when it came to meeting new people. The more times I set these things up, the better I got at it. I could go into a strange campground and within 2 hours of arrival have met at least 3 or 4 kids to start the weekend with. I used to love the shy ones. At first, when you talked to them they would not give you the time of day. I used to help them through the hard times of getting to know people. I remember a few kids that at the beginning of the weekend would not talk to anyone. By the end of the weekend you could not get them to shut up. I have two younger sisters. They would love hanging around with me on camping trips because they would know by the end of the first evening I knew most of the kids camping that weekend. Over the course of my childhood I bet I met hundreds of kids that ended up being close friends by the end of each weekend. I had some failures during this time, mostly with girls, though I was good at meeting both girls and boys. I would on occasion fall in love with one of the girls I would meet. I was very much a romantic in my youth. I believed in finding a girl, getting to know her and giving her flowers and holding hands and kissing. Most of the girls I met liked the "I ain't sissy enough to play with girls" type of boy. I had both success and failures with girls at that age. When I was thirteen my life went for a big change: My parents got a divorce. This has a direct effect on my self-image. For a long period I would not meet new people. I was put into counseling for my change in behavior. It was a neat program put on at Ball State University by students studying to be psychologists. They helped me realize that the divorce had affected my self-confidence and they helped me rebuild it. I went to these sessions for about two years. I would get a new student every semester and have to go through the whole story again. The repeating of the stories made me deal with it and made me open up to talking to new people again. When I was fifteen, I got involved in auctions. I worked as a ring man. For those of you who do not know what a ring man is, it is the person standing in front of the crowd looking for hands to raise for bids and reporting it to the auctioneer.

At first I was a little backward in this, not having the confidence in myself. After a while I resorted to my old self and not only took bids, but played with the crowd and had fun doing it. I would get to know new people each week. I would work flea markets on the weekends. This is a direct public position that required you to get people to stop at your booth by being a good talker. This is experience that I would use a lot later in life. When I turned nineteen, I got married to a girl I met at the auctions and moved to Houston, Texas, with her. I held several different jobs until I got involved with a furniture company. They had a mall store and I went to work for them. This was right up my alley; in the first three months I worked for them I sold more than all the other salesmen in all the mall stores this company had. One day about three months after I started the owner of the company came down from Austin and gave me a new mall store they were opening about sixty miles outside of Houston and paid me to move there. It was a real boost to my ego. The store was an island in the middle of the mall. My sales were OK, but being in the middle of the mall, customers thought it was a "here today, gone tomorrow" type of store. After about a year the company called me up and told me that they were going to shut down my store. After that, I moved back to Houston and they gave me a small outlet on the southeast side. After a while they called me again and said they decided to franchise my store and sold it to a private owner and told me that my services were no longer needed.

Well, that was a big blow; about the same time my first wife decided that she was homesick for family in Indiana and up and went home. I spent a couple weeks in depression. I had a whole series of girls I would date and drop. Or be such an asshole they would drop me. I really was getting even with all of them for my wife leaving me, and my boss letting me go. I finally got a job with an office supply; that is where I met my second wife. We had my first child in Texas and we moved to Connecticut to be with her family. Things were going OK, but I was not going anywhere. I was working for a McDonald's as maintenance. I don't know if you have ever worked fast food, but it is a jungle. You have store managers, shift managers, assistant managers and the rest were all of us who had no self-esteem working for them. That is where I got involved in going back to college and worked my way out of it. Now I am a president of my own company. Granted we are still small but getting bigger every day. The reason I dumped all this on you is for you to realize that you can change your life if you really want to. In this book I am going to tell you how I did this change. If I can do it, so can you!

Chapter 2
Why People Are Not Happy

In this chapter we will be looking at some of the reasons why people are not happy. It all starts at childhood, all the programming from our parents. Some of you will say, "I can't even remember most of my childhood." Your conscious mind may have forgotten but your subconscious mind never forgets. Locked away in you subconscious is all the experience you have had since conception. Every win or failure you have ever experienced is there. All the happiness, hurt, fear, depression, joy, everything. Most people I know are not happy because they long since decided that life is not turning out the way they wanted it to. Most people do not want to blame themselves when it is much easier to blame others. For a long time it puzzled me why I wasn't happy. I had a good job, a family home and what most of us consider being pretty successful. Instead of enjoying what I had, all I could do is to dwell on what I didn't have. A lot of us like that we have a roof over our heads, a car to drive, but what do we dwell on? The next-door neighbor has a bigger house, a nicer car and more. Instead of enjoying what I had, I was dwelling on the fact of what I didn't have. This isn't something you realize and then you know it forever. I still have that problem from time to time. Now I know it is OK to think about those things but not to judge myself by it. What I mean is just because the neighbor next door has more than me doesn't mean he is a better person than me. It is that he has better opportunities to get that house. Chances are he did more or worked harder to get in that house. This is not a reason to put yourself down. You can have anything you want if you are willing to prepare to have it. Here is what I mean: There is only one thing in your life you cannot change, and that is your past. The present and future are all up to you. If you want, it can be a poor one or a great one; it all depends on you. If you are comfortable with the way you are now, there is nothing wrong with that. If you are not comfortable with yourself then only one person can change that, and that is you. Remember, every day is the beginning of the rest of your life. If you have a bad day, that is OK.

Just as easy as turning a page in this book, tomorrow, you can do some things that will make it a great day. I will talk about this later in another chapter. You and only you can make the decision that today is a great day and I am going to make it count. You know, most people live their lives one day after another, not changing anything, and expect their life to get better; it doesn't happen. Remember this: If you live each day and don't change things about yourself, you can't really expect your life to change. In order to change your life you must first change yourself. Changing yourself is simple but not easy. A lot of things in life you will find that are true. If you don't like the way you get along with other people, then change your attitude toward that person and they will change as well. It will not come overnight. Remember, this person is used to not liking you; it will take some time to get him/her used to liking you. A lot of people are comfortable with not getting along with people; these are usually people that in past experience with others. They might have had friends that were close that betrayed them.

Once that has happened, these people will not let themselves be close to others for fear of betrayal again. We have all had that happen to us in the past. It is easy to understand why they are the way they are. Different people react in different ways. You can take that input and guard yourself forever or you can take that and forgive them for their act. You know the funny part about this is that the person that hurt you is that way because someone has hurt them that way. Human behavior is that way. Some will take the way they are treated and turn it around so they treat someone else that way. These will also be the people that complain about being treated that way in the first place. If a person is hurt enough times they will put up a wall as a defense and hurt other people around them. I am sure you have seen this. Just think how nice it would be if people just treated people like they wanted to be treated. I am sure you've heard this before: You have been hurt by being nice to someone and they turned on you. You will say, I was good to him/her but s/he did that to me. Well he/she did that to you because someone did that to them. The chain reaction just grows and grows. This reaction can be regional or family oriented, or just this person. We are all emotional animals. Our behavior is not instinct, but taught. We learn to treat people like we are treated. As a computer programmer I wish that all people had a RESET button on their heads. This would allow you to clear their memory and start with a fresh boot up. If a person is short tempered, it is because someone has been short tempered with them. Do you notice in the office when you go to work, if you have someone in a bad mood, that bad mood will spread all over the office? It is easy to follow the moods when they are bad and good, versus being the outsider that is in an opposite mood. What makes a bad mood person even madder is running into someone that is actually enjoying their day when that person is having such a miserable one. You will find that person will try to provoke you any way they can to get you to join into their bad mood. I have had the following said to me: You wouldn't be in such a good mood if you were responsible for this, this, this, and this. Well, I have news for them. I am responsible for that, that, that, and that, and I am in a good mood. Is their "this" worse than my "that"? No, I just know that if I let it, my "that" could be far worse than their "this." I just don't let it be worse.

What I am trying to say is their "this" is the same as my "that." They are all responsibilities. When a problem comes across my desk, I just solve it or have someone help me solve it. I don't dwell on the problem.

Am I saying that things don't bother me? No. I am an emotional human just like he is. The difference is I can separate the emotion from the problem, and then solve the problem. One of the secrets to this is to respond instead of react. I will get into this in another chapter. This is true whether it is a work, personal, or any problem in life. A lot of times I have seen that people are so emotionally involved in the problem they can't even see the solution if it is right in front of them. One little trick I have learned is to use the step-back method. The step-back method works like this. When you are in the middle of a problem and you see yourself getting upset over it, just take one step backwards. This is when you pretend you are not the one involved in the problem. It is your best friend and he wants your advice on what to do. Tell yourself what you would tell your friend. This may sound silly but it works. A lot of times I have seen that a person in a problem will give great advice to someone else; when the same thing happens to them they react in a different way. I use this a lot with some of the people I help. An example is I had this girl who was living with a guy that would get drunk and beat her up. She would not leave him, no matter how many times she would get beat. She was crying one night just after she was beaten and I went over to talk to her. She said, "I just don't know what to do." Of course I told her she needed to leave him; that didn't sink in. I told her to forget that she was her. Instead of being her, she was her best friend. "As this person's best friend, what advice would you give to this girl? You know that she is unhappy and that she is living in fear of this person." She said, "I would tell my best friend that she deserves better and to leave him." I said, "Well that sounds like good advice from a friend to a friend." She agreed and found the courage to leave him. I see that this is the case a lot of the time. A person that gives great advice to friends gives very poor advice to themselves. This comes under the forest and tree theory. That is the basis of what the step-back theory is all about. If you are not in the middle of all those trees, you can see the forest. This is the same for problems that come across in life. Instead of problem—react, problem—react, problem—react; you should have problem—respond, problem—respond, problem—solution. By being your own best friend you will see that your advice in solving these "other" people's problems will come easier. I have seen over and over again, people that have great advice for others can't solve problems for themselves.

Dealing with Compulsive Complainers

One thing we all face on a daily basis is the compulsive complainer. I am talking about 80% of the people around us that all they do in life is complain. Everything they come in contact with is just another reason to bitch about. To me this comes from a general dissatisfaction of themselves that they can't deal with. What I mean is, this is America, land of the free, and the right to the American Dream. The American Dream is to do in life whatever you wish to do. When you were a kid, you were taught in school you can become anything you wish in life. When you ask a kid what he would like to be, he will say astronaut, lawyer, doctor, or some other famous occupation. You will not hear a kid say factory worker or garbage man or unemployed. People in these jobs as adults are feeling cheated by the system.

Who do they have to blame for this? They will say government, other people, poor opportunity. But when it comes down to it, they don't have anyone to blame but themselves. You and you alone have the ability to improve your life. No one else can do it for you. I mean, I worked a full-time job, went to college and was a father to three boys. My own motivation kept me going. Yes, I didn't get much sleep, and yes, my family had to do without me for a while, but now I can make a good living and we can enjoy the better things in life. Time spent to get a better education is time well spent. I kept wondering if all those days of four hours of sleep a day were worth it; well they were. Anyway, back to the subject of complainers. I have noticed in the past that some people are very comfortable being complainers. They have been complaining so long that is the only way they know how to deal with things around them. Besides if they complain about others that throws all fault from them onto someone else. In their minds the fact that they can't deal with something is a weakness. This weakness needs to be someone's fault, and since they do not want to take the responsibility for it themselves, they can just push it off on someone else.

Are you a complainer? If you ask anyone that question they will say no, then start complaining about people that complain all the time. Most complainers are not aware of their complaining; they have done it so long it is part of their attitude. You can do a self-test. All you have to do is to monitor what you say during the course of a day. Don't stop yourself from complaining that day; just count the number of times you find yourself complaining about something. You will be surprised I bet. Even a positive person will unknowingly complain about things.

My problem with this was sarcasm. I found a negative part of myself by my reaction of sarcasm. Being a positive person, it bothered me that I have such a negative attitude on certain things through sarcasm. Can I say that I have completely cured myself of being sarcastic? NO, this is something that I have been doing for 30 years, automatically. I work on it every time I feel a sarcastic remark that I would normally just say. I ask myself each time, OK, why was I going to say that? Then I ask, OK, why am I feeling this way? Then I ask, what can I do to not feel this way? This is thinking my feelings through. If you keep the following statement in mind, you will be able to deal with these things in a better way. All feelings are a result of your subconscious mind and electrical impulses that form the vision in your head you react to. In other words it is the way your subconscious visualizes a bad thought and your electrical impulse gives a bad reaction. Thoughts are reflexes; if you put your hand on a hot pot handle, your subconscious senses the heat, the electrical impulse goes to you brain, and your brain directs you hand to let go. This happens in less than one second. Well, anger is the same; you have someone lose their cool with you, your subconscious sends an electrical impulse to the brain and your brain directs your mouth to yell back. Once a negative thought goes in your mind, it will react in the same way that you have reacted in the past. You can change this reaction in steps. First when an angry person yells, just before you yell back, stop and think. OK, why am I yelling at this person? Just because they are yelling at me.

Well, they yelled at me just because earlier someone had yelled at them. It is like a chain reaction. A lot of people just end up a victim of emotional chain reactions. Here is a small story I heard to show you how it works. John Smith got up in the morning to go to work; he woke up late and had to hurry. While getting ready for work, in a dead run he stubbed his toe. Driving to work in a rush, his foot hurt in all the way to work. On the way into work someone pulled out in front of him and he had to apply his brakes with this aching foot.

Well, by the time he got to work, he was really mad. He gets into his office; his phone is ringing off the hook. It is the plant manager yelling at John because yesterday's production had to be scrapped due to a wrong setup on a machine. So John walks out to the machine operator, who is a good employee that very rarely makes a mistake, and John with an aching toe gets more pissed off with every step. He gets to the machine operator and starts to totally lose his temper with this operator. Well, the operator sits there through this browbeating getting madder by the minute. After a minute or two of John unloading on him, John walks away in a huff. Well, now the machine operator sits down and starts to think to himself. "I cannot believe John did that. I am out here every day, working hard putting out a good product for years. I mess up once and that is the way he reacts. I should just quit this stupid place and they can hire someone else to take this." All day long this machine operator is thinking and getting more pissed off as the day goes on. At 5:00 he punches out at the time clock, pushing his fellow employee to the side. In a fit of anger he takes out of the parking lot squealing his tires. On the way he cusses out every car that dares to get in his way. Once home he kicks open the door and growls at his wife about what is for supper. She explains she had a busy day with the kids and running around, so she was going to just warm up some leftovers from the night before. Well, he lays into her about how he works all day while she just lies around doing nothing, and can't even cook him a decent meal. Well he pops a beer and goes into the living room to watch TV. Well she stands over the hot stove warming up the leftovers, saying, "I cook and clean and pick up after him every day for the last 20 years. I cannot believe he does not appreciate what I do around here." While she is busy getting all worked up about this, her son comes in the back door from his friend's house and asks, "What's for supper...?" Well, he should have just said, "Here I am. Will you please just yell at me?" Because she unloaded on this kid about if he would spend more time cleaning up after himself she would have more time to make supper for his daddy. Then she grounded him to his room for the rest of the night. The kid goes to his room, saying, "I clean my room and take out the trash and mow the lawn and I don't do anything? That really makes me mad." He gets into his room, slams the door and jumps on his bed, just getting so mad. He yells and screams for a while, and when he is done, he looks at the end of his bed and there is his smiling teddy bear. He looks at the bear and yells, "You just sit there and smile while I get yelled at all the time. I hate your guts." He tears off the head of that smiling bear. As you can see this whole thing started with John that morning and lasted the whole day involving directly 3 more people and indirectly involved the people that were all around those people. You know it would have been a lot better if John got up in the morning, drove over to his employee's house and went into his son's room and ripped that bear's head off himself.

See that bear's head did not get torn off that night; it was torn off that morning as soon as John got up late for work. The rest were just the steps to get there. You know it is nice to know that a chain reaction effect works that well. Here is why I say that: If a bad chain can be formed, well, it stands to reason a good chain can be formed. Since the brain thinks like a reflex, it can react in a good way too. As a computer programmer we have the saying: garbage in, garbage out. I am so happy that is true because that means if good's in, good comes out. If you can take in the good from other people, you give out the good to other people. Every day you run into people whose sole purpose that day is to tear off the head of your kid's teddy bear. Why? Because last night someone tore his kid's teddy bear. Each person can play a role in this chain reaction by responding to that teddy bear killer with a grain of salt, and stopping that negative energy right there. Am I saying never get mad about things? NO, this is something you cannot help but to do. But you don't have to pass it on. I have spells when I am upset. I just think about the reasons I am upset and do something about the cause, not the people involved. Once you learn about curing the cause, you will be able to handle anger. Think about it. The causes of anger are the only way to manage anger. You cannot do anything about the people involved in this chain until it is to your link. This is when you can end it. The best way to do this is to take in the anger of another and with a little sympathy try to get to the reason they are trying to kill your teddy. Once this person realizes why they are in teddy-killing mode, they will usually run out of steam. Now, I know what you are thinking: some people don't want to run out of steam; that is what keeps them running. Well, that is true. I have seen a lot of people that are driven by steam.

If they have a big job ahead of them the only way they can complete this task is to get pissed off enough they get motivated to do the job and get it done. Not that I am knocking that; motivation sometimes is hard to find. But if we need to get pissed off to get us motivated, wouldn't it be nicer just to get motivated? Motivation is not something you have, it is something you get. We used to have a periodic event that happens at my house. My two youngest kids share a room. The middle child will not clean up his room because he says the littlest is the one that makes the mess. The little one will not clean up because my middle child will not help him. What ends up happening is the room gets messier and messier.

After a while, their mother would get so sick of looking at the mess she yells at them and in a total rage goes into the boys room and cleans it. After that the cycle starts all over again. What can be done about this? Lots of things. Have the kids clean up their room before mom gets pissed off. I ask my kids, Do you like Mom yelling at you? They say no. Then I ask, Why don't you clean your room and then Mom will not get mad over it. Some people are so used to the cycle, bad or good, they do not want to give up the cycle. So, the kids just go on doing it. I ask their mother to work with them on getting their room clean and she says they wouldn't do it right anyway. See she is so used to the cycle she doesn't want really to change it. A lot of the time that is the case. When you have set ways you react to certain people, this is part of your back history with that person. Have you ever noticed that certain types of people you are around are quite a bit alike? If you look at some of your friends you will see traits in all of them that are alike. These are most likely traits that you have and want to see in your friends.

I have one friend who every time we talk we insult each other. Each one of us know that we are doing it but don't mind because we are taking a genuine interest in each other's lives. I go out of my way from time to time just to tell him that his friendship is special to me. That is when he will get serious and tell me that my friendship with him is special too.

Then we will go back to the comfortable act of insulting each other. Is this a healthy friendship? Yes, I think so. For one thing we can tell each other how we feel about things. A lot of men have that sort of relationship with other men. They really like that person, but being male we have the macho image to uphold. So, men will resort to other ways of telling friends how they feel about each other. This is a pattern that is hard to break. With my friend, we insult each other as a way of telling each other that we like one another. You know that we will insult each other when we are talking, but when we talk about each other to others, we give a lot of praise. To me having a relationship of this type with someone is OK, as long as you tell him from time to time how much you appreciate his friendship. A lot of the time men can't really express to other men without feeling uncomfortable about it how much they like another man. If a man likes a girl who is just a friend, he can openly tell her how much he likes her. When men talk to other men, we have this male ego thing that won't allow us to really express our true feelings for that person. I work on that myself with my friends. I tell them that they are special and I appreciate their friendship. This sometimes makes the other guy feel uneasy, but that is only because he is locked into the old male honcho thing and can't really express to you his feelings for you. You know when a girl likes another girl as a friend they can express it by hugging. I think this is a sad part about being a male. If I could hug one of my best friends and tell them how I felt about them being my friend, we could be a lot closer friends. But even I will not break the pattern and do this. I would feel totally uncomfortable doing it. Why, because of my programming. In my opinion males are the losers because of this. I have very close friends that I have lost because of little misunderstandings that if we were closer would have been able to work out. Is this something I can change? Sure. Like I said before, I would feel uncomfortable hugging my best friend but shaking his hand feels OK. So when I see him I always take the time to shake his hand and greet him with a smile. This is as far as I can go without feeling uncomfortable. Even to me this is something that I can change but will not. Is this wrong? I don't think so; if I was to lay a hug on my friend it might make him feel uncomfortable and would affect our friendship. I do go out of my way to tell him that he is a special friend and that I enjoy his friendship. That is where we can make a difference.

By going out of our way to tell this person how much you enjoy their company and friendship, we can help that friendship grow without the hug. You know a male would not think twice about hugging a female that is a friend and that hug means so much to that friend that may not have things going right for them at the time. You can do the same for your male friends by listening to their problems and telling them that you care about these problems, and shaking their hand. That is almost as good as a hug. To some of you this might seem weird or even a bit on the homosexual side. But that is programming in action. Whether your friends are the same sex or not has very little meaning. You still have the same feelings for them. Deep down you don't like to see them hurting. This has got to do with the male ego syndrome that I will talk to you about later. Well, enough about that; here are some things that will help in dealing with the compulsive complainer.

Step 1—Listen to the problem.

Most complainers are complaining for the sake of complaining. What I mean by that is you will listen to the problem and if you have a solution to the problem, they will not want it because then the problem is solved and they have to go to all the trouble of finding something else to complain about. So, when you are dealing with a complainer do not attempt to solve the problem. Attempt to solve the source. The source of the problem in most cases is that they are unhappy. When talking with a complainer, sympathize with their problem at the time. If you do not sympathize with them they will just find someone that will. If you want to really help the person, sympathize with what they are complaining about and help them to understand that this is a real problem. Offer a suggestion on what they can do about it. Then talk about all sides of the problem. If you can help them think about the facts of the problem instead of the problem itself, a lot of people will concentrate on the problem instead of thinking about the solution to the problem. It is like the forest-tree theory again.

Step 2—Bring out the good things.

A lot of complainers complain because they are seeking attention. You can give them the attention they want but do it in a positive way.

There are several ways to do it. You might try giving an example of a similar problem you had and how you handled it. Be sure when you do this not to just add to the problem. This is what I mean: Complaining is compulsive. If the person complains about something it will start a seed around his friends that when you are with that person you will find yourself complaining as well. Make sure when talking about your problem and your solution you tell it lightly, like it was no big deal. Remind the complainer about the things he has taken for granted. Every one of us is so caught up in each moment of life that we tend to dwell on the "I can't" and "I don't have" instead of remembering how well we do have it. I will talk about this later in the book more. Remember this: For every problem in life there are two sides to the story. It will help to show the other person both sides of the problem. It will help them focus on the problem itself instead of all the details of the problem. Here is what I mean. For example: Think of a problem as a wall in front of you. You come to the base of the wall; a lot of people will just sit there and say, OH, here is a wall in my way and I can't continue on my way because of this wall. It will stop most people dead in their tracks. By focusing on the problem you do the following:

Looking at the problem.

1. OK, there is a wall in the way.
2. What things will I need to get past this wall?
3. Where can I get these things?
Gathering the materials for the solution.
4. OK, I can get a ladder from the garage.
Taking action
5. I go to the garage and get the ladder.

Now you might say all problems are not that easy. You are right. But when the formula for solving problems is followed, solving the problem will be easier every time. You will find some people that do not want solutions to their problems. If you solved the problem they have to go to all the trouble of finding a new problem. That sounds silly,

I know, but it is a truth in life. Remember the compulsive complainer isn't really upset with the problems; they just need something to complain about. This is due to the programming that they have had all their lives. Negative builds on negative, meaning that this person is so used to being negative, they do not want to look for the positive. This can be corrected, trying to bring out the positive points when they are on that negative road.

Step 3—Taking action for a problem.
The following is the formula for solving all problems.

    A. Thought…
        1. Identify the problem.
        2. Identify the tools or things needed to solve the problem.
        3. Identify all the sides of the problem.

    B. Action…
        1. Identify what action is needed to solve the problem.
           Note—Sometimes the action is something that is not available for you. You will then need to think of alternate actions that will simulate the action that is needed.
        2. Follow through with the required action.

    C. Solution…
        1. Once you follow thought with the action the problem will take care of itself.

Remember that when it comes to problems some action is better than no action. You will find that some action may give you only a partial solution. It may not turn out the way you wanted it to but at least something was done about it. The reason is the person is not focusing on the problem; they are focusing on the solution.

Life Hardships

As most of us know that have been around this world there is a lot of negative thinking out there. Why is that? Well, there are lots of reasons. One is the life experience that you have run across. All of us have had times in our lives that it seems nothing is going right. You know when things go badly it seem sometimes that things just get worse. This is the old "when it rains, it pours" theory. Well this is a very true saying: On sunny days we don't worry about the rain. On rainy days all we do is worry about rain. The same is true about your life; when things are going negatively everyone will focus on the negative and the more you focus on negative the more you notice it. I am so happy that is a true statement. Why? Because if that statement is true the direct opposite would be true as well. When you focus on the positive you will see the entire positive about life as well. You will find people that are so wrapped up in the negative and even when positive is staring them in the face, they will find the negative points in it. Is there something wrong about these people? No, not at all; as a matter of fact it is really the standard behavior for most people. This is where you can really make a difference in your life. Be a positive finder. There is plenty of negative in the world, I agree, but there is just as much positive if you know when to look for it. Remember, you are the only one that can change yourself. What do I mean by that? Good question. The best way to explain it is in a computer term GI/GO. This is the computer term Garbage In/Garbage Out. Think of your mind like a computer. Everything in life that is inputted through your sense is your input. Sight, smell, touch, all of your senses are like the keyboard of a computer. This is how your receive input into your central processing unit: your mind. When you bring in the negative of life, meaning bad-tempered people, bad attitudes of others and everything else that is put out by the negative side of the world, it is taken in by your mind and processed then printed out of your mind by your actions to others. The good thing about all of this is that if you let the good input in you will process it and turn it around. But you might say, what do you do with that bad input that is everywhere? Well, this is what I do. First identify it as what it is. You will hear that negative comment and instead of taking it in, turn it around to positive as it goes into your mind. I know—Martin, you lost me…Well, every negative thought has a direct opposite positive thought. Remember for every action there is a reaction. You can change the thinking of a negative person by first sympathizing with their negative thought. If you do not show sympathy you will lose them in a minute. Bring to light all the good sides of the situation. If there is not a good side, just bring up something that may relate that is positive. Some things are very negative that you will be confronted with in life. Just remember the good things about life. For all of us, we tend to concentrate on the negative issues because we take for granted all the positive things that don't make waves. Think about it this way: If you stand in the ocean at the beach you have the series of waves hitting you. You forget all about the ocean you are standing in because it is still, and only think about the waves that push against you.

As compared to the vastness of the ocean that one little wave is nothing. But because it is hitting you, you will notice it. All I am saying is notice the water around you. Meaning each of us has lots to be thankful for. We have a job; we have a roof over our heads; we have people that love us. Some of you will read this and say, "With that and a quarter I can make a phone call." Well, you are right, but without that, whom would you call? Think about it…Each day of your life is a wonderful thing. If you don't believe that just try missing one. You have the power every day to make it a good one. I will talk about this more later. Life is wonderful, considering the alternative. Believe it or not, we are supposed to enjoy life. What I am saying is, we were all put here for the same reason: to be born, live, reproduce, and die. Out of these four things we have control over two of them: the live and the reproduce part. Reproducing is an option, of course, but living your life is something you have direct control over. As a matter of fact, you are the only one that really has control of it.

You can live and be unhappy or happy; it is your choice. You might say, "Happy, how can I be happy with all these problems I am having right now?" Well, problems in life will always be there. It is like breathing. How you deal with these problems is the control you do have. Remember, you can let problems get the best of you, or the best of you can get to the problems. This lesson we all forget from time to time. You might ask, "Martin, are you saying that life problems don't get you down from time to time?" NO. If I said that, I would lie about other things as well. Problems do get to me from time to time.

I have just trained myself to look at the problem for what it is: just a problem, not a life. Problems in life have solutions. Once you separate the emotion from the problem itself, you will have just the problem. Well, because it is just a problem, it will have just a solution. The solution may not be there instantly. But thinking it out you will come up with the steps to solve it. If a problem is so big and so overwhelming as some things in life are, you will need to talk to someone about it. Someone that is not emotionally involved with the problem. If you can't talk to anyone about it use the step-back method I talked about early in my book. All problems have solutions. Sometimes the solution might be something you don't like to do. But that action will be required to solve the problem. Each one of us has the power in us to overcome any problem we come across. Due to the bad input that we have received in life you may not think so. But you do have that power. Later in this book I will show you how to find the strength you have forgotten you have.

Chapter 3
How to Be Happy Every Day

Every day! I can hear you now. If you had my life you wouldn't be so perky. The only thing I can say is yes, and it is going to get worse. You might say, "Martin, that isn't very nice." Well, let me tell you why I said that. Each one of us does have the power to have a good day or a bad day. See, whether the day is good or bad is based on each one of us to decide what kind of a day it is. What I mean is, if the world blew up in a nuclear blast that would qualify as a bad day for everyone. If that doesn't happen, then it is all your choice whether it is a good day or a bad one. The choice is made out by your emotional mind. I have a very important experiment I want you to do now. First put your right index finger in your right ear. Then put your left index finger in your left ear. It's OK, just lay the book on your lap. Next I want you to look straight ahead of you. Go ahead, I will wait…Ok, now keeping your fingers in your ears, what you see in front of you is NOT what determines a good or bad day. The thing that is located from your right index finger to your left index finger is. Sorry, that is the only way I can think of to get this point across so you will be able to break the trend that all of us have.

We come across problems in our life and we allow that one event to mess up an entire day. You and only you have total control over that event and the rest of the day. You can either decide that event has made it a bad day, or you can respond to the problem and solve it then if possible, or put it to the side for later. Once you have solved or set to the side your problem, you can go on with the rest of the day and forget that problem and decide that you are going to have a good day. I know— "Martin, are you telling me you never have bad days?" I can honestly say yes. Why, because I do have some bad events that happen from time to time, but that is just a bad event that happens in the course of a great day. I know—"You are stretching it a bit, aren't you?" Yes, most people's standards would say I am. But most people I know are upset about stuff 50 % of the time. I am not claiming to be a master of my emotions but I am not a slave to them. In each of us there is the power to find a happy medium that will allow us to feel emotions and not be controlled by them. I find a lot of the people I talk to all the time are spending all their time thinking of the bad things in their life. I say, why dwell on them? Dwell on the positive things about your life. I know— "And what is so positive about my life?" That fact that you are alive to ask that question is what I would say is the best reason of all, considering the alternative. As Zig Ziglar would say, "If you don't think days are not special, just try missing one." That to me sums it up well. Each one of us is alive, and we have people who care for us, depend on us, to be there. All of us forget that from time to time. I do not have bad day, just an occasional bad event, which I deal with the best I can and go on.

"Martin, are you telling me that you don't get depressed?" If I told you no, I would lie about other things as well. I have days where everything builds up and starts to get to me. What do I do? Well, you're going to love it. Once I feel like everything is too much, I make a decision to be depressed. I tell myself, OK, Martin, apparently you want to be depressed so be depressed. I will give you till 11:00 to be as depressed as you want. Then after that is over then you can smile and go on. This may sound silly, but it works. As a matter of fact 1/2 the time I do this I can't even be depressed till the time that I allowed myself. I tell this to people all the time: I am busy being depressed; I will be over it at 11:00 and not a minute sooner because I have worked very hard for this depression and I intend on enjoying it. The next time depression sets in, try this method, and you will find yourself laughing about your depression. Now, don't get me wrong; chronic depression is a different story. You will need help for that. You know there is nothing at all wrong with seeking some help with your emotional problems. That is being strong enough to admit you need the help. Well, I am strong enough, at one time in my teens I had to get help.

Let's talk about a day. With most of us it starts with the alarm clock going off and us hitting the snooze button. After we hit the snooze button we will lie in bed and what is the first thought that comes into our mind? God, is it morning already? I just went to sleep. That right there is enough of a thought to ruin most people's day. Some that are a little better, will at least get up in a good mood, but by the time we get ourselves ready and think of all the work he have to do that day, we will lose that good mood even before we get out the door. Well, don't worry if you make it out of bed and get all the way out the door and even to work; there will always be someone at work that will set you off. Why, because he didn't even make it past the bed part. Now you might ask how I stay in a good mood. Well, that is simple: I just don't get into a bad one. This like a lot of things in life are simple but not easy. I do something that I would like all of you to do for one week. If you will try this for a week, you will see big changes in your life. First when the alarm clock sounds off, don't just lay in bed. Get up. Spend a minute to think about your life and see all the good in it. Look out the window and see the sunshine, take a minute to listen to the birds sing. Remind yourself that you have a job; some people are waking up with no job, no money, no food. As you are going into your morning thing getting ready for work, most of us take a shower. Showers are great in the morning because it starts the day with a clean attitude. I think about the shower as cleaning all the dirt and bad thinking off of me, so I can start the day with a fresh attitude. Once I am done with my shower I get dressed, and come downstairs. I get me a cup of coffee and turn on the news. I usually watch the local morning news; they bring across some of the more cheerful stories. If there are stories about murders or deaths, I turn it around by saying to myself, "Now that is a guy that wished he had another beautiful day ahead of him." Well, he doesn't and that is sad, but you do have another wonderful day to wake up to. Remember that each day is wonderful. Life is really short and we must make each day count. That is the way I do it; each day I do as much as the day will let me. I spend time each day to bond with friends, make new ones, and spend time with the ones that love me the most: my children.

For each of the people that die in a course of a night and make the news the next morning, you owe it to yourself to make each moment in life count.

Once it is time for me to go, I wish each of the kids, with a smile, to have a great day at school. Then I leave for work in plenty of time to get there. I drive at a normal pace and get there a couple minutes early. I want to stop a minute to talk to you about car driving time to work. Little does everyone know your time spent in a car is empty time in life wasted. Most of us spend 1 to 2 hours a day in a car. That time is time that is wasted, which can be used in more productive ways.
Here are some things to do during this time:

1. Join Automobile University. This is using the tape player in the car to learn things. Every week I plan what tapes I am going to listen to that night. Every day on the way to and from work, I listen to tapes. Usually on Fridays I will on the way home listen to music on the radio. It is my present to myself for learning all week.

2. Plan your day at work. When you are all alone in the car, it is a good time to yourself to think about what you are going to do and plan the order of things. When you plan your day and follow the plan, it will help you get all you want done more efficiently.

3. Plan your evening home. This is just as important. A lot of us lose time parked in front of the TV all evening and don't use that time to get things done. I am aware of this problem because I am one of the worst at doing this. I will get home and fall in my easy chair, turn on the tube, and watch. Ask me the next day what I watched. I wouldn't even be able to tell you. Because I have the habit of just sitting there and watching, whether I am interested or not. How do you fix this? It is simple: When you are watching TV, if something comes on that you are not really interested in, go and do something else. I spend time at my computer. You will need to find something to take up your extra time you are going to have.

4. Talk to yourself. You might say, "That is crazy, Martin. I don't talk to myself." Well, tell me who is the one person that can help you through feelings and direction of life? That one person is yourself. Everyone needs to really get to know themselves. I have seen it time and time again that something earth shattering will happen in someone's life and the person will deal with it and later say, "I didn't know I had it in me." I will talk a little later in the book about getting to know yourself.

These are some of the many things you can do with the time you have to yourself. I know with me that this time in the car is the only time that I am only with myself. When I am at work or with clients or home, I always have people around. Each of us has that time to yourself each morning and don't realize how special it is. Now let's talk about once you get to work; you have the power within you to have a good day. It starts with walking in with a smile on your face. The work will come in keeping that smile on your face. That is done by reminding yourself all day long that you are in a good mood. Everyone and their brother will remind you that they are in a bad mood, so you just remind yourself you're in a good one. You really do have to do it all day. The reason is simple: When you are dealing with bad attitudes all day some of it will rub off on you. But just remember you took a shower and all the bad attitudes that happened the day before are washed away. If you find yourself getting in a bad mood it is because someone else's attitudes are rubbing off on you. Have you ever noticed at work that when one person has a bad attitude the attitude will creep into all departments of the office? Well, the way I think about it is that after my shower I used some deodorant to keep me protected for the day. Well, little does everyone know that deodorant will also protect you from bad attitudes if you believe it. If someone comes into my office with their bad attitude rubbing all over the place, I just think, "Man, am I glad I used deodorant today, or some of this stinking thinking would make me smell as well."

Remember, that guy's misery in life is looking for company. And I will not keep company with it. This doesn't mean you have to get away from that person; you have to dust some of the dirt off of him a little so his deodorant will kick in. Something that I have learned is that if you always tell yourself you're in a good mood, you will be in a good mood. I know—"Are you telling me, Martin, you say you are always in a good mood all day? No, but I always tell myself I am and once I remind myself I am, I become in that good mood. You must remind yourself all the time. People around me would love to see me in a bad mood. Why? Because most spend one half of their life pissed off and hate it when someone is actually enjoying life. Everyone can enjoy each day if they would just decide to; it is that simple. I always hear, "I am in a bad mood because of this or that." Well, the "this and that" of the world are just events. Once that event takes place it becomes history. After that event you have a choice for the rest of the day to either enjoy it or not to enjoy it. I have seen people that come across an event that will happen in the morning and they will remain pissed off all the rest of the day and into the night, and some, the next day, and some, the rest of the week. You have the power to stop this trend. Once the event happens just deal with that event. Take a deep breath and finish the rest of this wonderful day. Each moment of each day is important; we pass through the course of a day without even thinking about it. There are people out there that will love to foul up your whole day. They will do that event and go on to the next person. The funny part about this is that person will go from one person to another, creating events to making everyone around them as pissed as they are. It is the snowball effect. It will start at the top of day with a snowball, and rolling down through the course of the day, it will collect all the snow it can.

That is why people are the way they are; each day they are collected into the negative energy of others and from that point on they are just rolling with the snowball. While they are rolling they will collect all the people that are in their circle as well.

Let me show you with an example how that works. OK, I am at work. One of my suppliers promised me a product by a certain date. The worker goes to do that operation and there are no supplies. He will get upset because his boss is always on him to get the job done. He will then go to the area supervisor and bitch him out that he doesn't have the part. The area supervisor will go to the plant manager all upset because of the line worker. Now let's review. So far we have 2 or 3 line workers, 1 Area supervisor, and a plant manager that is upset. The plant manager will come to me and say, where is this supply? I will get on the phone to the distributor and get on his case about the supply and he will call the Factory Rep., and the Factory Rep. will call his plant manager and that plant manager will call his supervisor and that supervisor will bitch at their production people. Now remember that each snowflake caught in this snowball has people that they encounter during the course of the rest of the day. Well, that is just one little problem from my end. If you take everyone's little problems and all the people that get rolled into each snowball, it is easy to see why people have the attitudes they do.

What I will talk about next is how to get along with co-workers. This is easier than you think. First of all you need to learn a little about yourself. At work there are several things you might be facing, things like gossip, backstabbing, and petty jealousy. These are very negative things. The one thing to remember is, a gossip needs someone to tell it to, someone to care about it. Remember this: Gossip about you needs you to care about what they are saying in order to be effective. If you do not care about it, it is just talk in the wind. As soon as it starts to bother you, that is when gossip affects you. The best way to overcome gossip is not to feed it. Meaning don't get caught up in the gossip and defend yourself. Just take it for what it is: idle talk from people that don't have anything better to talk about.

The next subject I will talk about is backstabbing. Backstabbing is an ego-related problem. Meaning that the backstabber needs to put other people down to build themselves up. You know a lot of people will, if they know who the backstabber is, turn on them and return the deed. That is all wrong. The only thing you should ever do behind someone else's back is pat it. If you always make sure you praise others when they are not around you don't need to worry about backstabbers. They are only doing it to try to gain points with other people. The funny part about this is that a backstabber is only really hurting one person, and that is themselves. Backstabbing only goes so far, because after they have backstabbed enough people, the other people see them for what they are. If you build up other people they will give up on the backstabbing that they do. The best thing to do to a backstabber is to help them build their ego and self-esteem in other ways. After a while they will not need to do the back-stabbing to feel better about themselves.

Jealousy at work is something that most of us deal with on a regular basis. A lot of times jealousy is caused by upper management treating one employee better than another. Well, sometimes this is true; sometimes it is not. The jealousy is just another snowball waiting to happen. Here is what I mean. If an employee gets upset because one of the other employees gets along with the boss better than he does, well, that feeling makes him more distant from the boss and creates hard feelings. The longer this goes on, the further from the boss this person will get. He will turn into the bad apple in the bunch.

He will talk about that other employee to others and make everyone dislike the employee. Now remember the only sin of the employee who is getting along with the boss is that he had a good attitude and is personable. If the employee who gets jealous would just spend his thoughts and energy to getting along with the boss instead of destroying the boss, he would not have the problems he does. Everyone should learn to get along with others instead of working on destroying; they should become builders. Build a good relationship with the boss and you will receive the benefits of it.

Next I would like to talk about the snowball effect I was talking about earlier. I am so glad that snowball effect works. Why, you might ask? Well, if it works for the negative then it only stands to reason it works for the positive as well. In a course of a day, you have a great power within you. When you are dealing with problems you can be the deciding factor in the rest of the snowball direction. Whether you are at the top of the hill or in the path of the snowball, it does take you to keep the ball moving. I want to take a minute and think about this. Picture in your mind a big hill. On one side of the hill is the positive point of view. On the other side is the negative point of view. Well, when you're dealing with people you can either start the snowball on the negative or the positive side. What determines this is your attitude. Whether you're at the top of the hill, or in the middle of the path of the snowball, your attitude can determine which side of the hill your snowball will roll on. Some negative snowballs need to be stopped by you. Others you can just send it down to the other side of the hill.

There is something else I would like to talk to you about that falls in the snowball effect. When you are at work have you ever noticed that when you make a mistake you will spend time worrying about it and make another one? This is like the snowball effect, only you are the only snowflake. You get so caught up in the mistake you don't think about what you are doing at the time you are doing it and you make another and another. You can stop this trend by first forgiving yourself for the first one. When I make a mistake (Well, this is hypothetical because I don't make mistakes [hehe]) I think about the mistake for a moment, and I think about what I could have done to prevent it. I think about this not to wish I had, but to do the next time. Once, I think about what I could have done and find the solution. Then I spend a minute to see what I can do to correct the error. If there is an action that I can do, I do it. If not, I just put it to the side and go on with the rest of the day. If there is some action that I can take to correct my error I do it then. After that set it to the side and go on with the rest of the day. Do I just forget about my mistakes? NO, they are very important. The mistakes we make are learning tools. What I mean is our entire life we spend learning from mistakes that we have made in the past. If you have a trend to forget them, you will make them again. Take responsibility for your mistakes; you own them. You can either dwell on them, or learn from them; the choice is yours.

Once you are finished with your work day comes the best part of the day; when you go home to be with your family, time is very important. I spend my evening talking to my kids, when I have them, seeing how their day went.

I would like to plead guilty of something. When I work all day and with clients after work, some nights I don't get home till late. I walk in the door and my kids want to visit with me but I feel like I just want some time to myself. Wanting time to myself, I had a habit of not really listening to my kids and what they had to say. At times I would tell them even to go away. Well, any parent would understand what I mean: I love them, but need some quiet time.

Well, I have found a way to have both. First, when you get home plan on spending a few minuets with them, and you will find that all they really require is a little of it and they are on their way. If you take a few minutes to visit with them and talk, it makes a lot of difference. Then after you have your visit time they will go and do their own thing and you will have the quiet time you need. Love for kids is spelled T-I-M-E. Spending time with them just talking and getting to really know them will help you with the times you have to be the father or mother and discipline them. I will talk more about this in my chapter on parenting. At the end of each day I do the following that really helps me. First I write in my journal. This is a computer journal that I designed to allow me to write, like a diary, my thoughts for the day. Do you really know what this is? It is my self talk. I can put into the computer my thoughts, which, when I do that, I am in touch with myself, on how I feel about the events of the day. Remember, each day is filled with events good and bad. By reviewing the events in a step-back approach, you can see that event as only an event in a course of a day. Life is so very wonderful, you get to go out and do your job, then come home and be with your family or if you are single with friends. Your daily self talk is very important. Because this is where you can look at each event in a day and think about the impact they had on you. Something to keep in mind is your mind is a processing unit for all your senses. What I mean by that is everything you see, smell, touch, taste during the course of a day is taken in. It is your mind that determines whether it is a good or bad experience. This is where you can make a big difference. You can learn to reprogram your mind by thinking about the positive. All day long you are confronted with the negative of other people. You can turn these events around and see beyond the emotion into the facts of the event and learn to deal with it on that level. I recommend that each one of you either start a written diary or a computer one. If you do not want to do this just put a time aside each night and think about things that are happening in your life. Each one of us takes for granted an entire day that just passed by. Did you make the most of it? Here are some questions you should ask yourself at the end of each day.

1. Did you tell the people you love that you love them?
2. Did you spend the day making friends, not enemies?
3. When you were at work, did you make it a good, productive day?
4. Did you do something to progress your goals in life?
5. Did you keep yourself in a good mood most of the day?
6. Did you spend the day spreading your good mood to others?
7. Did you learn from your mistakes?
8. Did you forgive yourself for your mistakes?
9. Did you spend some of the day educating yourself?
10. Did you take some time for others, helping them in their life and happiness?

Something to keep in mind: You will not be able to say yes to all of these every day. But if you can say yes to them more than you say no, then you will be living each day really well.

I want to spend some time on self talk. Your self talk is very important. This is a good way for you to really get to your deepest feelings. Some people are afraid of their inner feelings. I know— "Martin, are you telling me that I am afraid of the way I feel?" Yes, I am afraid that is the truth; we all are. Deep inside of each one of us is a person each one of us barely knows. It is our inner self, our "soul" if you will. It is the thoughts that we have that are the way we really feel, not the ego translation of the way we think we feel. I know—"You lost me, Martin." OK, here is what I mean. Remember early I said that your brain is nothing but an information processing unit? Well, the information that your brain processes comes with a hidden program. The hidden program is all the past experiences you have had since you were born. Every event in life is experienced through your brain as a thought pattern that references experiences before. A good example of this would be thinking of a lemon. If you have tasted a lemon before and someone cuts one and asks you if you want a bite, what comes to mind? The sour taste of the lemon. So after that, every time you see a lemon you will think of that sour taste. Well, this same reaction happens for everything else you do as well. Every event during the course of a day is referenced in your mind from an experience you have had before, not what you are really feeling about it. The real feeling is made on a subconscious level. That is where true feelings are created before they go through the past life experience program. Self talk will at first be with your ego program; then if you learn to dig a little deeper you will find the inner you. You might ask, how do I dig deeper? Well, the best way to find out how you really feel about things is ask yourself questions. What I mean is this. First, if you are upset over something, do the following:

1. Ask what am I upset about.
2. Ask why that upsets me.
3. On the response to # 2, think about why you said what you did.

Once you learn to follow this plan, you are on a new adventure to really learning about yourself. When you are self talking do it in a non-emotional frame of mind. Think about your feelings and think about why you feel that way. Self talk helps us deal with our feelings and therefore help us deal with life.

Getting Along with Other People

In this section of the book, I would like to talk about getting along with other people. This is where you get to play with your ego a little. Learning why you like or dislike someone will tell you a great deal about yourself. Each of us have certain people we like and dislike. This is a fact of life. Understanding the personality of these people can really help us get to know ourselves. In the Mayan culture hundreds of years ago there is a legend of the story of life. In the story of life there are 6 great characters.

1. Innocent
2. Orphan

3. Martyr
4. Warrior
5. Wonder
5. Magician/Shaman

Each one of us has these 6 characters we all play during every moment of our day. We change characters as needed to best suit the environment we are in at the time.

Let's spend a little time to get to know each one.

Innocent—Innocence is what we are all born with and carry throughout our childhood. This is the person that is unaware of the people and world around them. They just react to the moment based on the information that is provided at the time. To me this is the time of your life when you are not aware of the ego and just react to life with the simple feeling; at the time next to Magician it is the closest you will come to the inner you. It is the time of life all past experience is built from. You may ask, "Martin, do you have innocence when you are an adult?" Yes, at the time you try new things in your life you will start off with innocence.

Of course this is not true innocence because you have tried new things before and have past experience of trying new things. You will have only one time of true innocence; that is the moment of birth. From your first day on, you learn that if you cry someone will come; if you smile you will get attention from adults. This is all the building of past experience that will later control your emotional behavior and your ego.

Orphan—Orphan is a form of self pity that all of us fall into from time to time. When you get the feeling that you are never going to get what you want, that things never go your way, if I do get ahead a little then it will just be taken from me. You take very little action in this story for feelings of failing no matter what you do. This story is a great avenue for low self-esteem. Your ego is at a point where it learns to give up on things that are important to you. Your ego will give up a battle or a challenge by telling you that you can't win, so why try?

Wanderer—Wanderer is a very common story that involves us in just going along with everyone. This involves very little action, with the knowledge that everything will work out the way it works out. Playing the wanderer will require you to put your ego on the back burner. Being a wanderer from time to time is a good thing. It will allow you to understand not being in control; of course this means that someone else's ego is in control. You might ask is this a good state to remain in. No, it is not. If you are in wanderer, you will become victims of other people's egos too much. If you stay in the wanderer state too long you can lose yourself.

Warrior—Warrior is a story that there is no emotion involved. When you are in warrior there is a winner and loser period. You are going to be the winner. Warrior is the state where your ego is the strongest. This is one of the most powerful stories there is. Due to life experience you have been on the losing end of warriors; this is what fuels the power needed to have the drive to win. I have seen many times where someone in a warrior state will do anything and everything for the sake of winning. Warriors use non-emotion drive to overcome all that is in their way. The important thing to a warrior is not the issue at hand, just winning the conflict. This is why you will see people fight for something that is totally out of normal reason to win. At the time of winning it is a feeling of accomplishment. This, most of the time, is a hollow victory. It is hollow because the person allowed his ego to take over, to win. Sometimes, the warrior is useful because if you truly believe in the cause and you are up against a warrior, then to win you must use the warrior in you to win. This is OK, as long as the thing you are fighting for is truly important to you and the win is not. If you win in this manner it is not warrior state.

Martyr—A martyr is a person that will get a job done no matter what the cost is to yourself. I spend a lot of my life playing a martyr. I work long hours so I can provide for my family. I make lots of self sacrifices all the time to make others happy. I use this as a means to get what I want as well. If you look at your life you will see that you play this story as well from time to time. A martyr will always put the importance of others before themselves. To me the martyr is like the warrior in the sense that we want to win, but in warrior as I said before you have no emotion; it is a winner and a loser and you are going to be the winner. To a warrior winning is important, not the matter which you are fighting for. To a martyr the matter is important and you make a self sacrifice to gain the end result. A martyr will let the warrior win as long as the end result is the matter at hand gets done. Most of the time this is done by doing it yourself. A person that will say, "If I want it done right I have to do it myself." What you are really saying is, "If I want this task done, I will have to sacrifice my time and effort to get it done." When you look deeper into this, it is a form of self pity. Without saying it directly you will feel PLM (Poor Little Me). If you ever feel you are the one that always has to do a task or it will not get done, you are a martyr.

Magician/Shaman—Magician/Shaman is a higher state of awareness. This is the state of being aware of all the stories and at the time of need call upon them in a controlled manner to use them as tools. A magician/ shaman can see beyond the problem itself and not be controlled by one of the stories to react to the problem, but use the stories to find out others in the problem and what story they are playing and find a solution. The best way to play the magician/shaman is to use the step-back method of looking at the problem.

Now that I have explained all the stories of life that we all play every day of our lives, let's take an example to show how each of the stories would play out. Two friends are walking in the park together and at the same time they spot a $ 20.00 bill. Here is how each story would play out.

Innocents—Innocents would not apply because we have all spent $ 20.00 before.

Orphan—An orphan will allow the other friend to pick it up and not say a word about it because nothing ever goes my way and I wouldn't be lucky enough to find money.

Wanderer—A wanderer would let the other person pick it up and keep it all because $ 20.00 will not buy much and the wanderer really doesn't even care that they found it.

Warrior—A warrior will race the other guy to the $ 20.00 and claim that he saw it first. The $ 20.00 will not really matter, but he will want to keep it because he found it first!

Martyr—A martyr will either pick up the $ 20.00 and give it to the other or just let them pick it up. They will do this because the other guy may make less money than he does and could use it more than he could, or various other reasons that would make him feel that he needs to sacrifice his half of the findings.

Magician/Shaman—A Magician/Shaman would realize that the $ 20.00 found is nothing compared to the value of friendship. He would offer to split it with his friend. By splitting it, you will not offer it all to make the friend feel guilty. By splitting you will not keep it all to make you friend feel cheated.

As you can see we are all affected by these stories all the time, either through the giving or the receiving end of it. I know what you are thinking: It is best to play magician/shaman but how can I? The best way is to be aware of the other stories being played with you. Take time during a course of interaction with other people to notice first what story they are playing with you and then what story you play with them. You will find that certain people you will play certain stories. Once you realize the stories you are playing it will help you to understand how to get along with others. The best way to get along with others is through compassion. When you go out of your way to understand each person you deal with on a daily basis, you will begin to understand why they are the way that they are. You might ask, "What do I do about people that are impossible to get along with?" Yes, some people are impossible to get along with. Through their past experience in life they have developed a personality that is rude and offensive. When dealing with these people you will need to use more understanding of their attitudes and moods. You can do some good with these people, but keep in mind you are only a very small influence in their daily life experiences. It has taken many years to develop the attitude that they have. The small time they spend with you will not counteract for all the time they spend away from you. The best way is to learn about them through compassion and talk to them about why they behave the way they do. Keep in mind that you will not be able to change them in the short term. You may make some progress during an encounter and the next day when you see them they will be back to their old selves. If this person's attitude does not affect you too much, then you can stay friends with them. If their attitude is one that has an affect on you, you are best off to avoid that person. His attitude will affect you if your exposure to this person is continued. No matter how much of a positive attitude you have, a negative person in your life will play with your inner self to pull you to a negative attitude. As positive as I am, I have seen friends that can bring out the negative in me. With all the negative in the world it does not take much to pull you into it. If your close friend you depend on pulls you into the negative, it is hard to pull yourself out.

The best tool to help you with these people is just being aware of their negative attitudes and really thinking about the effect that negative thinking has on their lives and that you can point out to them positive times. This might cause the end of the friendship because as we all know misery loves company. Once you stop being negative with them they will become uncomfortable with your positive attitude and seek friends that are negative with them. Believe it or not, negative thinking requires reinforcement. Luckily there is a lot of negative reinforcement out their to keep everyone miserable for generations to come. Martin, is that a negative thought on your end? No, it is a reality thought; there is just as much positive out there as well if you learn how to see it. Every day you are surrounded by positive and negative; it is your choice which it will be. Everything you run across in the course of your life can be interrupted by your ego as a negative or a positive thing. Even things that seem positive are full of the negative. An example would be winning the lottery. Yes, this is a positive thing, but what will you think about, giving 1/4 to the government, relatives and friends who will be hitting you up for a loan, and tons more things that could come to mind? Why am I talking about all of this in a section titled "Getting Along with Other People"? Well, the answer is simple: You must learn how to get along with yourself before you can get along with others. Once you find the things about yourself that are not positive you will not project the negative on others.

Chapter 4

This chapter is the most important chapter of the book. The true key to happiness is to know and like yourself. Most of us have friends that we can get along with, but all of us from time to time can't be happy with ourselves. I know—"Martin, are you trying to tell me I don't like myself?" Yes, it is true, there is something that all of us have that tries to keep us from liking ourselves. That something is called an ego. The ego is the thing that dictates the actions of most everything you do. Every bit of guilt, loneliness, unhappiness, and all the emotions you feel are dictated by the ego.

Here is how the ego works. First of all you must separate the ego from yourself. I know— "Martin, the ego is me." Not really, and here is how. Ask yourself whose ego is it. Well you will think it is "mine." Well just like your brain, arms, legs, they are not you, just part of you. You can raise your arms and legs, so it only stands to reason that you can control your ego. Controlling your ego isn't a job that you can do and quit. It will be a job you take on for life. Wow, does that sound like a lot of work or what? Well, little do you know you are already doing it all the time, only with the power of the positive you will be able to do it and be happy. Remember, happiness is an emotion, an emotion that comes from the ego. You have been working on that ego from the moment you were born. Your ego's thoughts are not you. "You" had them; your thoughts comes from you "raw." It then is reference through your ego to look for a past experience to reference it and then it is thought. Here is an experiment to show you what I mean. First, clear you mind; now I want you to think about oooooaaaaaa mothballs. OK, what came to mind? Grandma's House, the closet at home when you were small. How about the smell that they make? I think you will see the point. You don't just have a single thought, you have that thought plus all the past references your ego can fill in. Have you ever noticed that when you are depressed you have bad thoughts that come to mind? When you are happy you have good thoughts.

You can be happy by just simply thinking happy thoughts. It is that simple, but like most things is not that easy. Each one of us goes from moment to moment and has to deal with all the irritations of life. Isn't life frustrating sometimes? Yes, it is if you let it be. Think about this: who is getting frustrated? Me, right? No, it is your ego; your ego is not yourself. It is just an image of yourself that you have. Let me say that a little differently. You are you; your ego is what you think that you are. With past experience, habits, likes, dislikes, your ego forms a picture of how to think about yourself, like the paper that is dropped into the tray of chemicals to form the picture. Well, the only real problem all of us have is that we are using the wrong chemicals. Most of us have far too many negatives in our ingredients. What you have to do is the take that pan over to the sink and dump the chemicals down the drain. Then carefully rinse the pan; we want to get out all of the negative. You might need a brillo pad (hehe…). Once it is nice and clean, put it back on the table and go over to the positive developer and fill up the pan to the tippy, tippy top. Don't worry if some of it spills out the side; there will be plenty of people you will encounter that need a little splashed on them. With the power of the positive in your chemical, you will only be able to develop positive pictures. If at the end of each day you dump out your tray. Each morning refill it and you can be happy all day. You know there might be someday you will have to dump it several times. Luckily, the chemical you need is always free. To help you learn how to get along with your ego, let's think about some of the parts.

Past Life Experience—Past life experience is everything you have experienced since the time you were born. All the things you think about now are reference to past experience. You don't touch a hot stove. Why? Because you think about the time you last did and burned yourself. The best example of this is the lemon story told by many speakers. First I want you to clear your mind. Then in your mind walk out to the kitchen and over to the refrigerator and open the door. On the top shelf is a lemon. Get that lemon and go over to the drawer that the knives are kept in. Open the drawer and take one. Put the lemon down on the counter and cut it in half. Then take each one of the halves and cut them in half again. Now take one of the quarters and pick it up. Can you see the nice yellow peeling, can you see the juice running off the sides? Next I want you to bring it up to your nose and smell it. Go ahead, I will wait…ok, now, look at it again and take a bite. Did you mouth water? Mine always does. This wasn't a real lemon but it was a real thought because my ego went into my past and remembered what it is like to taste lemon, and how sour it is, and then my body made my mouth water. Just think about it, if you have that much power in the non real, think of how much power you have in the real. Past life experience is the most important factor in the ego. We cannot change the past, but with our new developer we can run each of those thoughts through the positive to form the positive picture. To develop a positive chemical, "you," not your ego, must decide that no matter what happens you are going to be happy. Your ego will give you a hard time at first, but it will live. Remember, it is used to being in charge. Just like the bad weather that depresses you, certain people will just plain piss you off. That person is hitting on a past experience that you have.

Next I will talk about some of the emotions that your ego dumps on you from time to time.

Guilt—This emotion is a special one; it comes in many forms. It is the feeling you get when you don't spend time with the kids, don't spend time with your wife, Mom, grandparents, and much, much more. Guilt can also be with tons of other things as well, everything from not doing chores at home to overeating. Guilt doesn't even have to show up as guilt; it can hide in other emotions as well: anger, depression and many more. Think about it, if you get angry about something, the root of it can be a guilt feeling, that if I did what I was supposed to, this wouldn't happen. How do I learn to control guilt? Well that's the sad part. You can't, but you can forgive yourself. Think about this: all of us are willing to forgive a close friend for something he has done, but can't even begin to forgive us for certain things. Forgiving yourself makes you feel good. It gives you the good feeling of forgiving someone, and as a bonus, you get to feel good about being forgiven. You can forgive yourself by cutting yourself a little slack. Don't be so hard on yourself; know that you are human, and therefore you will make mistakes. A mistake in the past is a lesson for the future; I mean you didn't know that pot on the stove was hot until you touched it for the first time. The same is true for mistakes; you must make them to learn from them.

Loneliness—Most of you have all been lonely from time to time, right? Well, I would like to say I have never been lonely! WHAT, MARTIN? I know I should give a free pair of waders with each copy of this book. No, what I am saying is I personally never have been lonely; my ego has quite a bit. Just like a cut on my knee, I personally don't hurt because I am me and "my" knee has the hurt. I know—"Martin, you are starting to lose me." Well think about it this way. I own my knee. It is mine; it belongs to me. OK, who owns "me"? No one. Well my ego feels lonely and my ego belongs to me. I just have a little too much loneliness in my developer. You know it is a good thing that positive developer is free; this would cost a fortune to refill all the time.

Jealousy—Jealousy like other emotions is what I call a compounded emotion. Meaning it is made up of many different emotions: guilt, loneliness, anger, low self-image, and many more. Jealousy comes in many different forms: jealousy of a wife, being envious of a neighbor's new car, and more examples than I could possibly list. Well, it is time to crack open the bottle of developer and do it again.

Anger—Anger is one of the most deadly of all emotions our ego has. This emotion is one of the most important, powerful emotions that your ego has. This emotion is the raw fuel for your ego. It is the way your ego takes action. Your ego knows if you get anger about something that action will follow. Unlike other emotions like loneliness and guilt, these are something that you feel but very little action comes from it. Anger gets the job done. That is one of the reasons that people are pissed off a lot. Their egos think that the only way to get something done is to get pissed off and that is what sets the action in motion. I handle anger the same way I handle other damaging emotions. If I feel anger coming on I will ask myself, why does that anger me? Then I start to get to the root of the problem. This helps me learn about myself.

I would like to take a moment to talk about suppressed anger. Sometimes just finding the reason for getting angry isn't enough. Anger really needs an outlet sometimes. My kids know if Dad gets angry he means business. It takes that anger for them to stop their actions. If you use controlled anger, it is OK as an outlet. You might be asking, "Martin, what do you mean about controlled anger?" Controlled anger means using an authoritative voice and maybe even a couple of cuss words for effect and tell the person what you want done. This works with my kids; they know that Dad doesn't get pissed off very much so when he is they better do what they are told. Remember the rest of the world and all their lives they will be faced with people that will get angry with them. They need to understand that I have limits and once you have crossed those limits you will have to stop. Getting kids or anyone to stop their actions might require controlled anger. Otherwise, they will push that action on you more and more. If you do not react then you will suppress. Suppressed anger will either cause you to get ill or you will have a blowup of anger that is not healthy for your kids or others around you.

Now that we have looked at some of the ego-related emotions, you are most likely asking, "Martin, are egos bad?" No, they are just part of us. Some things about ourselves are not good or bad, just part of us. The worst part about our egos is that they are not really us, just a projection of whom we think we are. Now that you understand that, we can look at fixing you own ego to help you like yourself better.

Fixing the Ego

Now, as I have pointed out, your ego, like other parts of your body, is different from you. You can control the movement of your ego and make it work for you. Just like you would do if you raised your arm, you can move the ego to better work on being happy. Most of us are not in charge of our egos, but just the opposite is true. Is that bad? No, not really. Your ego has been in charge all of your life. It will have a problem with you taking control of it. Meaning that through the power of old habits you will have a difficult time with your ego. It is used to having its own way; like a spoiled child it will do everything possible to get its way. Now, I know what you are thinking: "Martin, if my ego has been in charge of me and I am not doing that bad, why should I change it?" Well, the key to the answer of that question is the "That Bad" part of the question. What I mean is that when the ego is in charge, it will have the feeling that you are happy on the surface. But if you look a little deeper in yourself you may find that you are not really happy. The best way to find out if the "me" part of you is happy is to separate yourself from your ego for a while to get to know the inner you. When you are in charge instead of your ego, you will notice some changed feelings. I did. Now, don't get me wrong; I am not in total charge of my ego, no one is. I just use some of that positive developer on my ego and move aside some of my past thinking to make way for some new ones. Here is an example of what I mean. I went through a long phase where I was not happy about with my second wife. What happened was my ego, when I first met her, formed an exact picture of what she was going to be like. Well, after a few years my ego decided that my wife wasn't living up to the picture it had created for her. That is when my ego started to tell me, "Martin, Yoooo hooooo; I am not happpppppyyyyyyy…" And my ego started to get upset with her over every little thing and my ego started to get depressed about it. I fixed my ego's problem with my wife by separating my ego's image of her and what she was really like. I introduced my ego to that fact that she is the way she is. Then through the power of positive thinking I taught my ego to be happy with her, good times and bad. Our egos are doing this same thing to us about every person and job and everything in life we come across. Our ego forms the picture of the way it should be and then adjust our behavior to fill in the picture. This is why we treat some people one way and others a different way. Your ego makes a split decision on whether you like a person or not based on past experience in life; then it spends the rest of the time filling in the picture. This is a very sad fact because a lot of times the person will not meet the requirements for the ego's picture and it will find fault in that person about everything. Not to mention the other person's ego is doing the same thing to us.

The best way to get control of your ego is to get to know it. When you encounter people and things all day, stop and think about the output that your ego is giving you. If someone upsets you, ask yourself, why is this person upsetting me? Once you answer that question, ask yourself, why does this action upset me? By getting to know your ego and the way it thinks, you are on the first steps in controlling your ego. The second step to control your ego is to be aware of the fact that your ego is the developer I was talking about before. If in your past you have had a bad experience with certain things, your developer will develop everyday activities into this bad experience. Just like when you go to touch something hot and pull your hand away, if someone you encounter during the course of the day has qualities of someone else you knew in your past, it will cause you to pull away or act differently. Take some time to think about some of your friends; most likely they all have basically the same qualities. Think about people you dislike; they too will have some of the qualities that are alike. Is this bad? No, not really, it is just part of life. The only reason I bring it to light is that our egos make a judgment on a person in the first couple of minutes we get to know someone. If our developer is full of bad past experience, we are unknowingly passing judgment on someone that may totally be wrong. That person deserves a chance to be himself, not your image of what they are. Each person is different, remember; there are not 2 people alike in the world. No matter how much a person reminds you of someone else, they are a totally different person. You may see some of the same qualities of one person and another, but they are different people; each person has his/her own developer that is based on their experiences in their life. The third and final step to fixing your ego is to reprogram it. Each time you meet someone new, don't use your first expression to judge that person; give them time to earn their own expression, then and only then decide their good and bad qualities before proceeding with the friendship. This is true with lovers as well. If you meet someone you are interested in give them a chance by getting to know them. I am sure that a lot of guys and girls are passing up the "perfect" mate for them because their ego labeled that person too soon. The next thing I would like to talk about is projection. Projection is a very little known part about us that plays in everything we do and say. Remember before I talked about the developer that is used to form the picture. Well, in projection your ego fills in the page with qualities that you don't like about yourself and finds them in others. I know—"Are you telling me that things I don't like about certain people are qualities I don't like about myself?"

Yes, very much so. If your ego is developing the picture, it is your image of what you do not like that creates the image of what you don't like. Have you ever noticed that certain things about different people bother you? Let us use an example, say, like lying. If you don't like a person because he lies, there is a part of you that doesn't like yourself because on occasion you lie about something. See, if the honesty in you gets upset with yourself every time you have to lie about something, it only stands to reason that if someone lies to you and tries to get away with it, your ego will get upset with them. The same is true about every action in life. If your ego considers someone else's action effective then it is using your developer to judge that person's action. Keep in mind that your ego is developing actions that others present to you. If that action is something that offends you, that is your ego telling you that you can't get away with that action, so why should they get by with that action? Another thing to keep in mind is that while you are projecting on others, others are projecting on you. I have a great way to show my theory. One day when you are having a great day and are happy and you run across someone who is negative, you will find yourself getting upset with that person. As well as that person getting upset with you, why? Well this is projection. You are happy and your ego is upset because this person is in a bad mood, and you're not letting your ego be in a bad mood. By the same token his or her ego is upset because it thinks that if I am upset how could someone else possibly be in a good mood. Now you might ask, "OK, Martin, I buy a little of what you're saying. What can I do about it?" The answer is this: You must take responsibility for that action. If something about someone else upsets you just ask yourself, why does that upset me? You will need to shut down your ego and look a little deeper to find the answer. Your ego will say to you, "Well it just does." You will have to look deeper than your ego for the real answer. The ego does not like to have to explain itself. It is not the real you, it is just the image of you. If you find that something upsets your ego, it is most likely because it is getting too close to what upsets you about yourself. Getting to know the things that upset you gets you more in touch with the real you and not the image you. If you start to get to know the real you, it takes power from the ego. Remember the ego is used to being in charge. By being aware of what upsets you and the real reason why it does, this is the starting point for dealing with why that upsets you. Many people walk around every day getting upset with people about things they do themselves. They never really rely that the person that they are really upset with is themselves. If you stop and think about the faults of others you have picked out that upset you, you will see in yourself some of these faults if you look deep enough. So Mr. Ego gets upset. This happens to each and every one of us.

I know what you are thinking—that I am full of buffalo chips—but when you start to really get to know yourself and your ego, you will find that it is all true. The key once again is getting to know yourself.

Chapter 5
Guide to Dating

This chapter is a guide to dating in the 1990s. Most people might ask, "Martin, you're a married guy. What do you know about dating?" I do have experience in this matter. I am the kind of guy who every girl meets and can talk to right away like a brother. I call this the BBS: Big Brother Syndrome. I guess it comes from having two younger sisters. I spent most of my childhood as a councilor to them and most of their friends. Now I work as a street corner councilor to most of the girls I know. They say I am easy to talk to. One thing I have noticed that being easy to talk to means just keeping quiet and listening. To start the guide you must first understand girls and guys. Ask any guy if they understand women and they will say, "Are you kidding? No one does." Well, I have news for you: Women are easy to understand. You just have to know a little about the way they think. Modern day women grew up in the fifties to the seventies. In the fifties Dad was lord of the manner. When Dad came home from work, he came in and sat on his chair. And the rest of the night was spent either drinking beer or smoking a pipe—"Father Knows Best" syndrome. Dad made all the family decisions and when Dad spoke it was law. The same was true during the sixties as well because a generation of fathers was still in command. New fathers of the sixties were still stuck in the crowd of the older fathers of the fifties. So if they didn't show a little of the Father Knows Best syndrome they were considered rebels or overaged hippies. The sixties to me were the turning point of fatherhood. You still had to maintain the lord manner, but you were allowed to get off the couch and do stuff. How many guys do you know that said twenty years ago, "If I start acting like my father, shoot me"? Well if we carried through on that promise, we would wipe out three quarters of the male population.

During the seventies things were progressing quite a bit, wives were more independent and the father still had the final word, but the women only came to the man when it was something they didn't want to deal with. The seventies were the time of "Wait till your father gets home." I am the father of the eighties and nineties; I get to do the lord of the manner only when my wife allows me. Granted, I still come home and sit in my easy chair and watch TV, but my children don't worry about being quiet around Dad or bothering him over any little detail they think is worth telling you. Now you might ask, "What does all this have to do with dating?" Everything! Ninety-nine percent of women are looking for a husband with qualities they had in a father. I find it is not as important with guys to find a person like their mother. Since the woman is the main factor in dating. The father syndrome is a major factor in dating for males and females. I call this finding a dick like dear old dad. If you ask a girl if what she looks for in a guy, they all say the same thing.

I want a guy with the following:

1. Sense of Humor
2. Sensitivity
3. Good Looks
4. Money

You ask any guy that is successful in getting girls. What is the number one way to get a girl interested? To act like you don't care whether they live or die. Most of you might say that makes no sense at all. And that is why you are confused. Well, that is how it makes sense. To follow, you must remember the following life rules.

Rules females follow:

1. If a guy is interested in me, he can't be good enough for me.

2. Sensitive guys are for friends only, not lovers.

3. If a guy is cold and distant, he must be hiding his feelings as a defense and once I break down the "wall" I will find a loving and caring person.

4. If a guy does not show interest in my problems it is because he is interested, but does not know how to express it.

5. If a guy flies off the handle all the time, it is because he does not handle things well.

Rules Male Follows:

1. If a girl is interested in me, she can't be good enough for me.

2. If you are interested in a girl, do not show it.

3. If a girl is not interested in me, this girl is a challenge that must be won to preserve my masculinity, whether I am truly interested in her or not.

4. Males do not openly talk about feelings with girls, unless it is someone you would not even consider dating.

5. It is better to be a taker than a giver.

Now let's take the time to talk about each one of these rules. First females. Rule one, if a guy is interested in me, he can't be good enough for me. Some girls that read this will say that is bull. But that same girl is most likely single and has a bunch of friends, mostly guy friends, that have from time to time shown interest in them, but she gives them the "I consider you a friend" line. Sometimes that means that you are not good looking enough, or don't meet one of the other requirements for the rule, but most of the time that means that you are interested in her; therefore you are not a challenge event; meeting someone and falling in love should be more like the movies. A guy and a girl meet, have problems, then overcome the problem, then fall in love. Usually this couple will fight or hate each other till the movie is over, then fall in love. Another thing you are dealing with is her dad and mother who have been married for years; Dad loves Mom but doesn't really show his affection in the public because the newness is all gone. This will cause her to feel like you're too clingy if you are holding her too much.

Now let's talk about rule two. Sensitive guys are for friends only, not lovers. If you line up 100 single girls in a row and ask them the five most important things they're looking for in a guy, every one of them will say sensitivity in one of their five answers. If you line up 100 truly funny and sensitive guys and ask them why they don't have a girlfriend, they will say because all girls like them like brothers. Again this relates to the family unit. Mommy didn't go to Daddy about her problems; she went to other females about it. So a male that is capable of being sensitive enough to talk about problems is not like dear old dad, and can't possibly make a good husband. I realize that me showing interest in a girl is not being a challenge, which keeps them from wanting me. I once had a girl that said to me, "I don't see why you keep flirting with girls all the time; you're married." Well, the reason I flirt is not to score. To explain this I will use the Coyote theory. As children, each one of us spent every week of young life watching the coyote chase the roadrunner. Now even though all of us rooted for the coyote, we knew that if he caught the roadrunner that would be it, no more cartoons. In other words, it is not the end result that is fun; it is the chase. The third rule is one of my favorites. I often talk about this one. I have seen, time and time again, a girl that meets a guy and the guy is a real ass. Of course the girl can't talk to him about it, so they come to me. They will say well, he has been hurt bad in the past and that is why he has that attitude. Well, I have yet to meet a person who hasn't sometime in their life been hurt really bad. Getting hurt is part of life. The guy, knowing that a girl likes the challenge of breaking down the wall, will put the wall up there in the first place. To not have the wall means you're sensitive enough to talk to her about your feelings. You know that most women complain that most guys are assholes. Of course they are: it is the best way to get laid. Most guys know if they show interest in a girl, they won't even make it to first base. Anyway getting back to the point, most of the time you will find the same asshole on the inside of the wall is the same asshole that was on the outside. There are always exceptions to the rule. To understand this you must know about the concept of basic nature. There are people out there who go through most of their life basically pissed off at the world. Most have set high standards for themselves in life and blame the world for not being able to make it to their self-appointed standard.

Some people find comfort in keeping a negative attitude. Basically, if you're pissed off most of the time you don't have to explain. But if you're away in a good mood then people want to know why.

As an experiment you can do to test this theory, for a period of one week, wake up every morning and from the time you wake till the time you go back to sleep, be excited about life. Everyone you meet greet with a big smile and tell them you feel great and let them know you are enjoying life; then count how many times people will ask you, "Why are you in such a good mood?" The funny part about it is if you act quiet and depressed then that is the norm, but if you're excited about life and love living it, people think that it is out of the norm.

The fourth rule: If a guy does not show interest in my problems he really is interested, but doesn't know how to show it. This rule can go either way. What I mean by that is being concerned about your feelings of course would be showing sensitivity and that is not allowed in the Masculinity code of ethics. I will talk about the Masculinity code of ethics later. A woman might say that he has so many problem of his own, he doesn't have time to take interest in mine. You know I was sitting at a bar once with a couple that just met; the girl was sitting there dumping her life out on the table to the prospective male and Mr. Sensitive says, "Well, that's your problem," and gets up to walk to the restroom. The girl looks at me and says, "Oh, that poor guy, he must really have some deep problems if my problems didn't even raise an eyebrow." I, being comforting, said she was probably right and left it at that. When the guy returned, the girl went to the restroom and the guy says to me, "This girl is totally messed up," and he wished she would take a hike. The point is that a girl, once she decides that this is the guy she is interested in, reads in all responses the way she wants them to be instead of the reality it is. One thing to keep in mind is that all of us, men and women, have problems. By working out our own problems we have the understanding to help other people with theirs. Another example of this is a good-looking guy I know; he calls his girl he is dating "sugar babe." The girl thinks he is so sweet and that she is his one and only sugar babe and that name is a term of endearment that shows her that she is the special one. Well, in reality he calls all his girlfriends sugar babe because he dates so many at once he can't keep the names straight.

Rule five: If a guy flies off the handle it is because he does not know how to deal with things. You know this is a funny one. Men are not supposed to be able to handle emotions as well as women. Well, here is a big secret I am about to unfold: Men have the same abilities to deal with feelings as women. Yes, I would not lie to you. Of course men aren't allowed to show it, but they do. To me a man that flies off the handle does so to get the women to deal with it. To understand this, let's do a scenario. A guy and girl are at a bar; they just met and are lining things up for the kill. (Sorry, the phrase "death do you part" has always applied that you wait till the other kicks off then you are free again.) Anyway, another guy comes to the table and lays a big kiss on the girl. Most guys would sit there pissed off until they lose their temper. By losing his temper, it forces the girl to react either by telling the other guy to buzz off, or leaving with him; either way he gets the job done. Of course it would have been better for the guy to tell the woman that this upsets him. But to do that would require him explaining his feelings. A guy knows that when his father got pissed off the family got into action. You know the funny part about it is that most people think we have progressed from the caveman era to become the modern people we are. It seems that some things like emotions and dealing with people have stayed somewhat the same. Back in the old west a guy that had a problem with another guy just shot him. Due to current laws, we are not allowed to do that but the feeling to do just that is still there.

Now we will start the male rules; some are the same as the women rules. This is a common ground to work from. Rule number one: If a girl is interested in me, she can't be good enough for me. This is true with both men and women, the feeling that a woman must be concerned to win the price of a wife. Most guys have the perfect woman for them right under their noses. But for one reason or another they have dismissed them as being a friend and not a lover. A girl's looks plays a big factor in this. If a guy dating a girl that is overweight or unattractive will be ashamed of this fact. A good-looking girl at your side shows that you are a real man that can land the girl of every guy's dreams. I compare this to the manly sport of fishing. If a guy lands a small sunfish you would think he would be happy. I mean, he is out fishing and he caught a fish; that is the whole propose of fishing, right? What I mean is the goal he has set of catching a fish has been met. If a guy catches a large bass even though it is a fish just like the sunfish, it is a better fish. Well, guys rate women about the same. If a guy walks into a bar, he will pick out the prettiest girl there and that will be what he will fish for. Even if the sunfish are jumping in the boat, he will be upset that he didn't catch the bass. Good-looking girls have fishermen throwing bait to them all the time. Girls that are not good looking are happy when a guy flirts with them. The funny part about it is that the non-good-looking ones usually have more personality and are easier to get to know. Getting to know a girl that has not been hit on all the time will get better results. You will be able to talk to them without worrying about the kill. Unattractive girls will usually have an easygoing personality to make up for the fact of their looks and appreciate you more than a girl that gets hit on all the time. It is funny to think that most attractive girls once they get married put on weight and let themselves go. The only problem is they will keep the "good-looking girls" attitude. What I feel sorry for is a good-looking girl that lets herself go then gets put back out of the dating market; they have to develop a personality to compete in the open market.

Male rule two: If you are interested in a girl, don't show it. Because you have to come across to a girl as a challenge you can't let a girl know that you care about them. This sounds strange but it is true. It would be nice if you could meet a girl and be able to let them know you are interested. A girl will not respond to this kind of approach because Father never really acted like he liked Mommy. Of course you knew he did but he didn't show it much in public. If a girl knows she can have you with little effort, what is the use of trying? Somewhere in history there came a time that if something is worth having you have to work for it to get it. I mean if car companies just gave away sports cars it wouldn't mean anything to own one. If a guy just gives himself to a girl without a fight, it will not mean anything to own it. This is where humans become possessions. If you wish to try an experiment, do this: go out to a bar where none of the girls know you. The first bar, every girl you talk to open up to them, let them know that you are interested in them and be open about yourself. Then the next night go to the same bar and talk to different girls, being very private and short. You will find that on the first night any girl you approach openly will lose interest very fast. The second night if a girl can't find out about you, it will pique their interest and they will seek you out to find out more about you. It is like a birthday present: If you get a present that is not wrapped you already know what the present is, but if the present is wrapped it will pique their interest until they get the present open. The funny part is you are the same present, but finding out what you are is the challenge.

Male rule three: If a girl is not interested in you she is a challenge, no matter if I am really interested in her or not. I have been out at bars where the guy I was with would hit on a girl that was very rude and didn't want a thing to do with the guy. By doing this she sets the stage for the challenge. This guy would try all night long to get the girl interested even if he had a table full of girls at our table that liked him. At the end of the night he would be upset because the girl didn't even give him the time of day. What is worse is the times that he gets the girl interested and he finds that this girl is a total bitch. All night long he has had girls that have been trying to get to know him, but the one that didn't want to know him is the one he will end up with, or go home by himself.

You may ask, "If I am out at a bar and see a girl I like, what should I do!" Well the best way to "land the bass" is to create the challenge for her to overcome. This sounds stupid but it is the way it is. Better advice would be to take interest in the girl that is interested in you. It doesn't really matter if this girl is not as good looking as the one you want; the fact that this girl is interested in you means that she will be easier to get to know and will turn out to be a friend if not a lover. Making friends with a girl is far more important than falling for some girl that you can't talk to. There is a school of thought that everyone should marry his or her best friends.

Male rule four: You should never talk about your feelings to a girl unless there is no way you would ever date them. Each one of us guys have met girls that you, from the time you meet them, can talk to about feelings and yourself. This girl is most likely unattractive or overweight. You can open up your most internal feelings to this girl because you know that you are not on the hunt and will not lose this girl. There are guys out there that will be upset for weeks about losing a girl that really didn't give a crap about them, but not think twice about the girl that is there to talk them through it. This is truly a waste; if this girl cares enough about him to allow him to dump his problems and feelings on her, she most likely cares for him a great deal. You know a lot of times this will work in the same manner as the girl you can talk to; she will consider you a friend only, and knowing that when she gets involved with a guy the friendship will end. I have had in the past girls tell me that they care for me so much that they could not take the chance of dating and ending the friendship. Yes, dating will end a friendship if you let it. That is because they think that once you sleep with them, you stop being a friend and start being a lover. Nothing really changes in this relationship; the caring is still there, but your attitude toward each other is different. This comes to a good question: If a girl is a friend that you can open up to anytime, why can't a lover be a friend to open up to as well?

Male rule five: It is better to be a taker than a giver. This is one of my favorite rules to talk about. In life and relationships you will find 99% of the time there is one giver and one taker. A school of thought is that this is necessary for a balance in a relationship. Look around at most of the couples you know. You will find a common thing about them. You will either have the male that is the taker, meaning that everything is the way he wants, and it is the female that caters to him, or you will have a female that is the taker and the male is the one that caters to her. Most of the time the roles are picked at the time of the first meeting. What I mean is if it is the guy that has to break down the girl to get the "kill," then it will be the guy that will end up being the giver and the girl will be the taker. If it is the girl that is the one that breaks down the wall then it will be the girl that is the giver and the guy will be the taker.

The Masculinity Code of Ethics

1. A real man enjoys watching sports on TV.
2. A real man does not talk about feelings.
3. A real man is good with tools.
4. A real man never needs a map.
5. A real man doesn't have any feminine traits.
6. A real man hates shopping.
7. A real man is lord and master of home.
8. A real man doesn't do what he is told to do by a female.
9. A real man only thinks about sex all the time.

If you're a man, you are influenced and expected by females to meet this code. If you don't meet this code you are not a "real man." Well, I have news for everyone. When you were born you were given a certain part of your anatomy that automatically made you a real man. As far as the code these are all ego related. Meaning, women expect this sort of behavior that is close to the way their fathers acted. The funny part is that their fathers acted that way for the very same reason you have to act that way. This is a trend that most likely goes all the way back to the caveman days. In England and France in the late 1800s and early 1900s, men started to explore the feminine side of their personality. It is a sad shame that this did not catch on. What I mean is instead of a woman expecting me to live by the code of masculinity, I could get a date by just acting like myself. If I were single, I would act as I act like myself; true this would not get me lots of girls, but the girl that learned to like me, instead of the manly image I project, would be the right one for me.

The Male Image
Women are very set on the way a man should act. They set into their mind the way they want things to be. Here is an example of what I

mean. There is a girl I know that dated this guy who from time to time beat her. She is all the time blaming herself for his actions. She finally breaks free of the guy by liking another guy that really doesn't like her.

This guy is the playboy type that likes to tease girls while dating another. He will show up with a date and sit all night long either arguing with her or putting her down. He has already had the "kill" so it is time for the next one. When the girl gets sick of being insulted she gets mad and leaves. That leaves the door open for my friend to enter into the web. My friend spends the first night telling the guy of the guy who beat her. The guy comforts her and for the next several weeks they meet at the bar with her not really sitting with her but just briefly talking to her a little at a time. This guy brags to the other boys that she wants him bad. The girl is alone with no one but has decided that this guy gave her the courage to leave the one that was beating her. Then one day it happens: The guy comes in with another "kill" and unloads her right in front of the girl, and he, in all his pain and suffering, gets the girl to sleep with him. Well, without telling the rest of the story, you should know how it ends: The next week at the bar the girl comes to the bar with that guy and for some reason unknown he gets in a fight with her and she leaves. This girl, to this day, still takes every chance to talk to the guy and go home with him.

He now tells his friends that she is a nympho that will not leave him alone. I got a chance to talk to her one night; she was mad that he just plays her along. I didn't go to the bar the next week, but the week after I sat with the guy who was telling me he "nailed" her again last weekend. Is this girl in love? She thinks so...

What Is Love?
Well this is something that will be a true mystery to most people. There is love for your family, friends, and lovers. You notice that most people think that love for a friend is different than love of a lover or family. The point is love is love no matter what or who it is for. Love is the happy feeling you receive when you are with that person. I have lots of girls that are friends. I care for them very much and they care about me. We enjoy our time together talking and laughing, in general

just being with each other. Is this known as being in love? No. Because why, sex? The only difference between loving a friend and a lover is sex. If you have sex with a friend, he or she stops being a friend and you love them as a lover. If you love them when they were friends, is your love for them as lovers different? Most of you will say yes, well why? Sex is a way to show affection. If you kiss a friend he does not become a lover; if you have sex with him he does. Here is a deep question: If you can have sex without love then why can't you have love without sex? Just think about it, a guy and girl that don't have sex get married because they just like being with each other. You know one of the funniest things I've heard is a girl that tells you if I have sex with you it will hurt our friendship. Most girls think this way, that the fact that they love spending time with you or talking to you isn't enough to make you a lover. As a lover you are missing the challenge it would take to make you a lover. She knows because no one on TV starts out being friends. Remember, love is love, whether it is love for your family, friends, or lover.

How to Find Miss Right

Well, the answer is right in front of you. In the way couples find each other, opposites attract. Have you ever noticed that if you have a girl who is nice and easy to get along with she will be with a guy that is a total asshole? And if the guy is the sensitive and caring type, he will be with a cold woman. Well to get the right one you will have to reverse the opposites effect. This will not be easy; you are breaking years of trends. You will find that acting sensitive and really caring will turn most girls off. Those girls are not going to be looking for you; they are looking for their fathers. When you find the girl that is interested in you when you are you, not the playing male image, this will be the one you should be with. Remember this girl may not look as good as the others, but what are looks when you have someone that loves you. Looks are external; it is the entire person that really counts. Most likely the girl that is right for you is right under your nose. It is the girl that is there for you when you are down. The girl that you talk to about problems and like to be with. If you do not have someone like that in your life, you should work on finding a friend that is that way. Remember this girl most likely will not want to be your lover at first. She will not want to break trend and be your lover. This is where you will have problems. I suggest you have her read this book.

The Energy + and - Factors

Plus Factor People—These are people that enjoy life and can open up to the people around them. They think of others above themselves.

Minus Factor People—These are people that don't enjoy life. The generally look out for themselves before others. Very self-involved people.

OK, as we know, everything in the universe is made of energy. Our body, our feelings, all energy. You may think a plus factor male with a minus factor female will balance each other out with the concept that for every action there is a reaction. Well that is not the final action. Meaning the action of + and - together has a reaction of + and + or - and -. If the normal relationship is + and -, which most couple are, then a + and + that don't attract each other most likely are most suited for each other. I mean, two people with a + energy will have a positive direction in their energy together. You might say that a +/+ relationship will have a reaction of -. Well, the reaction of - is already there because the + and + do not attract each other, therefore creating the - effect. To me the same is true about a - and - relationship, which will have a + reaction, but will have the - effect from + and - too. Another good theory is that every person has a + and - factor. Before you can have a good relationship you must first evaluate your + and - to adjust your energy to equal out. If you are a negative person you need to add a little positive outlook to your attitude. Most people in the world are on the negative side. That may sound harsh but it is true. Remember when we were all kids and we were told, "This is America; you can be what you want to be"? Well the teachers and parents around us would ask, "What do you want to be when you grow up?" I don't ever remember anyone saying, "I think I want to be a factory worker, or work in a McDonald's for low wages." Most of us had a little higher standard for ourselves. Now if this is the country that you can be anything and you end up doing something you hate, most people can blame only one person: themselves. But instead of a person blaming himself, he will blame the people around him. Well since that person goes to the job he hates every day that reminds him that he is not what he wants to be, generally his self-image goes, and he blames the world around him. Anyway, back to the theory. You must opt a + and - with yourself; then you can find another person with a + and - and you will both equal out and the relationship will work.

Dating Environments

Now we will talk about some of the dating environments. I guess the first one will be the singles bars. There are different kinds of bars that work different ways.

1. Country Bars (Small Town)—This is a very interesting environment. If you are a member of the town you will know some of the women that are in the bar, but worse they will either know you or know of you. This is one of the most lethal places to look for a mate. Most of the women in these bars don't like going long distance to look for men. You can about bet that if you pick up a girl in one of these bars you will either know someone she has slept with or she will know someone you have slept with. This could cause problems. I have found that most of the women that hang out in these bars usually do so to get away from their boyfriends, or husbands, to go up and have a drink.

If you dare approach this girl you will stand the chance of the boyfriend coming in or someone else telling the boyfriend that you were with them. The best thing to do if you are a guy is to go to a small town bar if you like the environment but NOT the one in your small town. Women in small towns like to date out-of-towners. Because most of them would love to live elsewhere, but have not the courage to do so. If you are a female the same goes true as well; being an out-of-towner, the male will be interested in you because you're not the same old girl that hangs up at the bar every weekend.

Most successful guys that go to the small town bars either have slept with most of the girls up town, or just plain turn them down. By being the "fresh meat" you will be able to get their interest. You might say fresh meat, which is a harsh term. Well most bars are just meat markets. Girls will say that is the way that most guys see it. Well who says that, the girls? So, in fact if a girl thinks a guy considers the bars as meat markets, but they go up there anyway, they are providing the meat for the market. In other words, if you go to a grocery store and all the shelves are bare, will you go back? No! If you go to a bar every weekend and there are no girls then you will not go after a while. Most girls will say they go up to talk to the girls and have a good time. Well in some cases that is true, but if a girl is up there all fixed up with makeup and nice clothes, and says they are just up there to have a few with the girls, chances are they are looking for male fresh meat and don't want to admit it. The meat market phrase applies to men as well as women. If you are a girl you have set up with other girls and checked out the buns on a cute guy. It is the same thing as a guy checking out the set of hooters on some girl that passes by. I, being the kind of guy that girls talk to, have been sitting at a table and good-looking guys pass by and hear all the talk that goes on. You think us guys are bad, you should hear some of the things they say: "Forget it, no bulge," "Check out his tight ass," etc.

2. Rock Bar (Small Town)—It is basically the same as country but there are some differences. The main difference is the kind of men that these girls are looking for.

They want the rock, MTV look in their guys. A straight-up, clean-looking guy will not have much success at these places. They are looking for the biker/rock-star-looking guy. Not that this is bad; this is what floats their boat. I suggest if you are a guy and want to "get lucky" in one of these bars you go there with hip looking cloths; you can watch MTV for ideas how to dress. The same is true for the girls that go to this bar. Look "hot" like the girls on MTV and you will not have any problems at all.

3. Country Bar (Large town)—This environment has some of the characteristics of the small town bar. Even in a large town you will have

your regulars that come to certain bars every weekend. Along with that will be the small town girls who like to get out of going to the local bar and meeting the local boys. Some of the girls in the larger town bar are approachable. Most are careful; they are aware of all the weird people in a larger town. They will be more open to meeting different guys but cautious. When you meet a girl in a bar, try to find one that is not too blasted.

If she is blasted, she might be one that has a drinking problem. Granted she will be easier to pick up, but that usually means that she has been easier to pick up for many other guys as well. If you are going to a country bar, you should not wear the traditional cowboy clothes unless your normal wardrobe is wearing these kinds of items. I suggest wearing jeans, of course, but wear a nice shirt and skip the hats and boots. Unless you regularly wear them, you might ask why? Well, it goes back to being yourself; a guy that dresses up for the country bar but his everyday clothes are something different then will put on a false front to hook the girl. If you like wearing these clothes when you go out to a bar, by all means do it; if you just dress this way to attract a cowgirl looking for a cowboy, you are putting on a false front and this girl will not last.

4. Rock Bar (Large Town)—This is usually an open market, meaning that rock bars will have some of the younger girls in it that one week will go to one place and next week will go to another. You should wear the MTV look and go light with the kill. Meaning you are just one of the guys up there to party; if you find a girl to talk to, don't get too deep at first. They are up there to party with friends and you should be one of the friends.

5. Topless Bars—This is a bar that I suggest that all single men go to from time to time. Do not go to a topless bar to "score," go to build your ego. You know at the single bars you will face a lot of rejection. In this environment, you must put aside the thought that these girls are working for money and enjoy the attention you receive. These girls know how to give you the kind of attention you need to build your self-

image. Remember, in these bars an ugly guy with money will receive the same amount of attention as a good-looking guy with money. This is a form of a meat market that every guy can enjoy and it can build your self-image and success with other women in other places. What I mean is you go to a topless bar, tuck some bucks and get some hooters in the face. Where in the single bar market can you get a face full of hooters for a buck? In topless bars you as the guy are in control. As long as you shell out the bucks you will get the attention. Some guys say, "I don't go to those bars because you blow all that money and end up alone." Well, how many times have you gone out to a bar, bought yourself drinks all night, maybe met a girl, bought her drinks for the rest of the night just to see her go off with some other guy or just leave alone? It is the same thing, money is money, so who cares if you're spending it for drinks for you and some girl or spending it to have some tits rubbed in your face. Granted, when going to topless bars you must follow a rule that I used. First of all, before you go in, set aside an amount of money to spend for the night. Only take that amount into the bar with you, unless you have good self-control. Once that money is gone, get up and walk out. But until then have a good time, don't worry about scoring with the girls; unless you have a couple hundred to blow, you won't get anywhere with them. Just go in have a good time and check out the nice hooters. You might ask how going to a topless bar will help you score with other women. Well, you must remember that an important part of attracting a girl is self-confidence. If a guy believes he is something worth having, then a girl will see that and want it. Granted there is overkill in this theory. Having self-confidence is not the same as being self-centered. You must keep in mind that when you go to the topless bar you can get away with behavior that you can't in a singles bar. You must adjust your attitude from the topless bar to the singles bar, meaning you can't expect the same kind of reaction from a girl at the singles bar as you get at the topless bar. But the fact that the girls that work topless bars are usually knockouts and they are interested in you is a real ego booster. Forget the money factor; I mean you work all day doing something you have to do to make a living and so do those girls. The ONLY difference is they make more money than you do.

Non-Bar Environments

Church—This is a common place for a non-bar-going people to find a partner. I have heard that the best kind of partners to find are at church. This may be true; not going to church very much I can't really comment. I can tell you to watch out for some of the people you meet at church. Some people that go to church are fakes. Don't get me wrong, I am not church bashing; it is that about half of the churchgoing people I know go to church every Sunday to make up for the hell they raise all week. At church and church socials the members will act differently than they do in "real life." I am not saying this is the majority, but some do. I do find that most single people do not attend church, unless their family is attending the same church.

Dating Services—This is a nice new way to meet people. There are various ways to contact dating services: through the newspaper, magazines, over the Internet and even the Dating Network on TV. This is something I personally recommend; you can meet girls and get to know people you can't meet in bars. When you try it, find a person and make friends with them first. Don't use this medium as the Home Shopping Network.

Use it to meet new friends of the opposite sex. You never know, one of those friends might fall in love with you. During my last divorce I met a couple of nice girls this way.

Grocery Store—Well, the hype has it that it is a "meat market" (pardon the pun) for the nineties. I truly believe that it is just "hype." I talked to many couples to see if any of them had meet in a grocery store and so far I haven't found any yet. I even talked to single guys to see if they ever dated anyone from a grocery store. Only a couple said they had but who knows if this is just ego talking.

The No Shopping Theory

This is a theory that I support: The best way to find a mate is not to look. I have seen time and time again a guy or girl that goes out every weekend and talks to people trying to make dates or just go for the kill. They will get so sick of it that they just stop looking; well all of a sudden they're dating someone. It is like magic. You know that if a girl comes on to you, as a guy you are saying, "Well, this girl is interested in me, but I wonder why she is out making the moves." Or if you are a girl, you will say, "Oh, he acts like he is on the make, and there must be something wrong with him because he has no girlfriend or wife." You know I think that a lot of guys fall into that void. If you act like you are interested in a girl and the girl knows you are interested, she rejects you because of it; you have just entered the Twilight Zone. Meaning, the guys who don't worry about meeting girls and just could care less about having some bitch around to ruin their lives are the ones who have the worst time getting girls to leave them alone. But a guy that is lonely and wishes he had a girl around him will have the hardest time finding someone to hang around. Well the idea from this is to not look for a girl to find one. It may sound confusing but it is not.

Some of you might be saying by now, "Martin, how should I act when I go out?"

What I have to say for that is do not go shopping. Don't have your credit card out; don't go to bars to pick up women. Don't put on a male costume and attitude to wine and dine a girl to hook her and then spend the rest of your life treating her like shit. You are just you; you have friends, you have family that you spend the weekend with, so you are not going out looking for a girl because you are going to meet a girl that will like you, warts and all (as the saying goes). You really don't want a girlfriend, you want a friend that is a girl; that is you get to know each other and fall in love. Am I asking for the impossible? We will see. You might ask, "OK, Martin, what about sex?" My answer: Your hormones are fighting you all the time to go out and get some sex. But sex is just sex. Wouldn't it be nice to make love to someone? You want to make love to someone for a change, and you can't make love to someone before you fall in love with him or her. So, put your hormones on the back burner and go on with your life.

Chapter 6
Being a Happier Person

This chapter is going to be how you can be a happier person in your life. In previous chapters I have been talking about getting more in tune with your inner self. This chapter will help you in dealing with your outer self. I don't know about you but I get tired of forgetting things. I don't know how you are; my memory skills leave a little to be desired. I try to combat this with a few things I have to pick up along the way. The first is my memo list; I used this for a while and it does help. The following would be an example of one.

Memos W/E—05/21/95

1. Work on client at home.
2. Kids' baseball practice (MON-6:00 7:30)
3. Call my dad.
4. Spend time working on book
5. Get oil changed in racecar.
6. Pick new right rear tire, racecar.

During the course of a week as I complete, I will put a check mark to the side of the line. If by the end of the week I did not get it done, I mark it with an "M" or an "X." "M" means Move to next week's list; "X" means to forget it. At the end of the week I will mark it, then write next week's and transfer all "M's" and add anything new. In order for this to work you must keep the list with you at all times. I keep mine in my briefcase or in my car on the weekends. As things come up during the week I will write them down on the list. This seems like a lot of work, but try it for three or four weeks at least. If it doesn't work for you, chuck it. One thing that will really help you in remembering things will be to talk to yourself. As I have pointed out in previous chapters, talking to yourself is good for you anyway. Each day you can remind yourself of things that are going on that day and help you remember. This works better than just trying to remember. One great point of organizing yourself is getting out of procrastination. I had always said, "I will stop procrastinating tomorrow." I am the king of procrastination. I am still that way; I will fight myself all the time to get something done today that I love to put off until tomorrow. You might say, "Well, Martin, how can you cure me of it when you have not even accomplished it yourself?" In my opinion this is something no one really ever totally accomplishes. Just some of us are better than others. I would consider myself middle of the road. I have my strong and weak times. At my weak times, I put more effort into getting things done. I notice that I usually run in cycles. Sometimes I am good at getting the job done that day; sometimes I procrastinate too much. At my weak time, I use delegation to get the job done. Some of us need a lot of work in delegation. We think that if it needs to get done right, we have to do it ourselves. This is not the case; you can delegate smaller items to give you the time to get more things done. The biggest secret to delegation is follow up. Once you have decided to delegate a job, just spend a minute to follow up and make sure it is done. Am I saying delegate everything? No, just the items that take up part of your day that someone else can take care of. This will help with your relationship with your kids and wife. If you show them that you are willing to share some of your tasks with them it will give them the feeling of being needed. Everyone needs to be needed. You know it is funny that when we have a task to do for ourselves it carries very little importance to us, but if we are doing something for someone else, it will carry a little higher priority. That is why delegation works. If I let my kids do something for me, this gives them the feeling of being needed and gives me the time to do other things that I might put off. I have a lot of people ask me how do I do it; I have a job, my business and a race team. I am busy seven days a week. Well, with all that going on I have learned how to delegate and follow up, and what I must do myself. In previous chapters I have talked about the step-back method of dealing with problems you have in your life. Well, the step-back method works for this as well. Once you can separate all the responsibility you have from yourself, you can get a better picture of how to get everything done without being overwhelmed by it all. Most of us get so caught up in our busy schedule, we do not see the big picture. It is easy to get caught up by the trees that are in the forest. By separating ourselves from the entire task we can get the task done as a director instead of getting it done as the worker. Once you direct the task and delegate what you can and do what is left yourself, you will find a lot more is getting done. This is how I handle it. Let's talk about some examples. I will start off with my race team. The parts of the team are the following:

Martin—Owner
Rodney—Mechanic/Driver
David—Pit Crew
Kyle—Pit Crew

I use this structure to delegate the work. Every week the owner is responsible to make sure all the parts come together to get us to the track. I have a mechanic change the oil and do any other work that needs to be done on the car itself. Each weekend I will have the pit crew prep all supplies that we take to the track and load the truck race day. The driver is responsible for driving the car at the races. Once you put this into place you can have a very good race team. If the mechanic is busy one week I will have David in the pit crew change the oil for the next race. If Kyle is not going with us I will have David do all the prep work for the race and the loading of the truck himself. You may ask, well, what do I do. I spend my time making sure all the pieces of the puzzle work. I am the one that will follow up and provide the money that is needed. My revenue from my business is part of what goes into the racecar budget, so by having clients, after my job I will help pay more bills and finance the racecar as well. I look at my business as my future. Working the business is fun for me, and building my future. I enjoy my regular job as well; even though I can quit my job tomorrow and make more money, I enjoy being part of a team that makes other businesses look good. There are other reasons I stay as well. Owning your own business full time is a hassle all in its own because my job and my business require me; I use a lot of delegation for the race team. See, my mechanic enjoys working on the car; my pit crew enjoys racing and feeling like they are part of the team. So, each of us is doing something we like to do and it works. When each one of us does what we like to do, all the tasks get done and we all enjoy it. That is very important because even though all this is work, to each one of us it seems like fun. Several times during the week I have a review meeting with all the parts of the team to make sure that all the tasks are being done; this is the follow-up part I talked about earlier in this chapter. You may ask, do I ever help with the racecar itself. Yes, on occasion when the mechanic is over I will help him with his work; sometimes I help the pit crew load the truck. As the director I am not there to be in charge at those times but as a helper. This is where your ego needs to be in check. Even though I am the owner and director of the team, when I am helping part of the team with their responsibilities I am just the helper. This way you do not undermine the importance of each part of the team. As far as I am concerned it is the mechanic that is responsible for the engine. He and only he makes every decision for the engine. As the driver he is responsible for the driving and handling of the car, and only him; he will make decisions on the tires. The pit crew is responsible for prepping for the race. Since David and Kyle are just kids, I will on occasions advise them on what to bring and what not to bring, but for the most part they are in charge of it. To me this is why it works. The director must know when to direct or when to stay out of it. I have seen in business too many times where the owner of a business will get involved in every little detail of the business, not letting each part of the team do its job. This is one of the worst things a director can do; if you undermined each part of the team, you will have a breakdown of the team. Only by letting each part of the team do its own thing will you have a successful team. This kind of approach works for other things as well, even in the family. What I mean: As a father I am a director as well, my wife has certain responsibilities, my kids have certain responsibilities and I have certain ones too. Each part of the team "family" does their responsibility and feels like they are part of the team "family." Of course dealing with kids you will have to do more follow up, but that is just part of your responsibilities as the director. You might think, well, if all of us are directors, that sounds like too many chiefs and no Indians, as the saying goes. This is not true; each one of us is a director of our own responsibilities. We are just part of a team but directors of our own responsibilities. Each one of us is part of the team of the life. I mean I own my own business, but I have clients (customers) that are in charge of their own responsibilities, and who have customers of their own. When you really think about it each one of us is just a piece of a big team, everyone from rulers of countries to owners of business to factory workers. Here is why a factory worker works all day to provide a product to the market place. That same factory worker earns his pay, gives part to the government to make the government work; that makes the economy work. That same factory worker will take the rest of his money and buy items that are produced by other factory workers. Each one of us plays an important part of a team; you might ask what the team's name is, and it is called life. We all live in our homes and use electricity and gas provided by some guy who gets out every day and repairs and maintains the lines. Every part of our lives is dependent on others in this world that are dependent on you to do your job. So whether you are the president of a company or a factory worker or in the food service industry, we all need each other to survive. Why am I talking about all this in the middle of my section on organization? Part of the reason is we are not all working on our organizational skills is the feeling of lack of importance for what we do. It is important for each and every one of us to work on the organization of our own responsibilities. This will help all life be more productive, but better than that it will help you. You will not feel so overwhelmed by all the responsibility you have. Spend each one of your days getting the most out of it. Getting the most out of each day most included spending some time to stop and smell the roses as they say. We all get so caught up in all of our worries and responsibilities that we do not take the time for ourselves. This is very important, for a director to keep your prospective on all the problems you have in the course of your life.

In this next section I would like to talk a little about accepting life for what it is. In the course of life we all tend to lose the big picture. We are all so wrapped up in ourselves that we tend to forget what life is about. You might ask, "Martin, what is life about?" It's simple; life is about living. Every time you take a breath you're having a successful life. It's when you don't take that next breath that you are really not successful at life. All the rest is really just details. What I mean is what kind of a career you have, what kind of car you have, what kind of money you make are all just details in your life, not your life. If a man loses all his possessions and goes broke, is his life over? It may seem that way at the time, but life goes on. You may have less possessions, but you still have that all-important next breath. The next step beyond life is quality of life. Quality of life can be measured by possessions or money, but tell me which man has a better quality of life, a man with lots of money and no friends or a poor man with lots of friends? Well, our ego will say the man with all the money can buy friends. Yes, on the surface this might be true, but are these friends that will be with you always, or just while the money is there? A true friend will be around when you're too poor to have a pot to piss in. They will offer you a pot. When you need something to eat and someone offers you a meal, that is a true friend. They offer this meal not out of pity, but because if the roles were reversed you would do the same for them. Like lots of other things in life having friends requires responsibility. It is not the kind of responsibility you do because you have to but because you want to. Even a poor man can be a good friend; you can't give what you don't have, so he may not give your money. He can be there for you with an open ear to listen to you or he can help you with something he can do that you can't do. I am a computer programmer; I sit behind a computer all day and get paid for it. I protest manual labor; you could not pay me enough money to do it. But I will do manual labor for a friend that needs my help. All people need others from time to time, and once you are in the practice of giving time, you will receive time. We all get so wrapped up in our little details of life, we forget to live. We forget to take time for friends and people we care about. This is very important; true friends don't require anything but your open ear and time. With my busy life I fall into trends myself where I find I am not spending time with my friends. That is when I change and start taking time. I will do this for a while and then go back to not spending time with them. Then I start the cycle all over again. The details of life will do this to you. It will pull you away all the time; it will be your job to pull yourself back in. Why do I do this, you might ask. Well most of the time the details of life that I am busy taking care of are important, I agree, but not as important as a friend. I know this because when I am busy working my business, this is important, but when my business is slow there is nothing there. When I invest time into a friend, when business is slow, I still have the closeness of a friend. You might say to me, "Martin, I am not very good at finding new friends." Well, here is an important secret I learned. When you go out to find friends, you will not be very successful. When you go out and be a friend, you will find them all over. You must take the time to start. I spend a lot of time "wasted" on people that turn out not to be a good friend. Is this really wasted time? No, not really because each time I do this I get a feeling of caring for someone else. You cannot make them return the care and if they don't, just go on. If they do, then you have just added another friend to your life. Life in general is the same way; the more you give, the more you receive. A person that does not give time to friends will not receive much time from them. A person that does not give time to a career will not receive a career. By devoting your time to all areas of your life, all the details of your life will devote time to you.

In my life I have made good money and sometimes very little money but I always have friends. This shows the importance of the time that I invest in my friends. I devote time into my children to receive the time they spend and love they have for me. I devote time to this book for the goal of getting it done. See, the time I devote to this book has many different receivers to it. What I mean by that is, my goal is to get the book done.

Another goal is to make my financial life better. Another goal is to improve myself and my attitudes on life. Another goal is to help others. If this book does not get published it is not a waste of time because I will have still reached two of the four goals. I will have completed the book, and by putting my ideas down I am improving my life. Who do you think is reading this book the most? It is me. In life, time is invested into many things. Some things that seem like a waste of time have other returns to it. You may think you are wasting time on something because you didn't receive the final goal. You will find that other return will more than justify the time you have spent. Even more, most of the time the other returns outweigh the main goal. When I finish this book and it sells, it will help my financial life, but once I spend the money it is gone. If you as a reader use some of this information to improve your life and help you enjoy it more, then which do you think is really more important? By the same token, if I use what I am talking about in this book to improve my life, once the money is gone I will still have a better life. Don't get me wrong, I am not saying the money is not important, just that the other is more important. I would like to spend a little time talking about MONEY. When it comes to quality of life, money is highly over rated. It is true that money is one of the most important factors in life, but way down the list of quality of life. A rich man with no friends and love in his life, to me, doesn't have much quality of life. Having someone to care and love you doesn't require money and it is the most important factor in quality of life. You know, it doesn't cost me a nickel to give a friend a hug or an open ear when they need it. These are the things that quality of life should be measured by, not how nice of a car you drive or how nice a roof over your head is. A man that makes $20,000 a year has a roof and a car. A man that makes $200,000 a year has a bigger roof and a bigger car. That is all there is to it. A small house full of love is far better than a big house full of emptiness. Don't you agree? You know this is one of the funniest parts about the last statement I just made. The man with the big house has spent so much time working so he can afford that big house, he will put aside the family and friends to do it. Once he buys that big house, he will be a stranger to his friends and family. So, what is left? A big, cold, empty house. Is this a life of quality? What if he goes broke and loses that big house? How he measured the quality of his life is gone. What if he, along the way to building the money for this big house, took some time for his friends and family? He might have had to settle for a little bit smaller house, but would have the love and care of friends and family. The funny part about it is, he can have it all if he wants. By devoting quality time to the career and to friends and family, you can have your cake and eat it too. There is where most of us fail. You find all the time career people eat, sleep, and drink their jobs. This is a great way to build a good career but not a good life.

You might be asking by now, "OK, Martin, how do I know if I have a good quality of life?"

Here is a mental experiment for you. First I want you to think about your life. Then take away your career. Then take away all your possessions. What do you have left? If you say nothing, then your quality of life is poor. All that stuff is just things. If you can say you have the love or caring of friends and family, your quality of life is great.

Some of you might say, yes, my friends and family love me but what else is there? My answer is nothing! The rest is all details. Think about this: If we lived in a world that provided everything for you without money, I would go to work to program computers for a company that remodels and paints factories that makes car parts for another factory that makes cars for another person to get to work. This is the way our lives work; only they put in a money factor for control. The factory worker and the president of that company both do the same function. They provide cars for others to get to work. The difference is the money control factor. The president makes more money and has more control. I wouldn't mind working hard because when I get out of work I have a nice car to drive home and I have a home. The money control factor is a very deep one and I will get into more in my last chapter. In this next section I want to talk a little more about having success in your life. Previously in this chapter I was talking about quality of life. I was a little hard on money and success. I did this to show you the difference between money and quality of life. Once you have spent the time to earn the love of your family and friends, it is OK to want more. I want more money, I want a bigger house, I want a nicer car, and I want a successful career. I have the love of my family and friends. Wanting all these things is not bad, unless you want them for the wrong reasons. What I mean is, if you want a bigger home for you and your family to live in that is OK. If you want that bigger home to impress your neighbors and friends that is wrong. Here is a good example of what I am talking about. Before I switched jobs one time I bought a 1985 white Jag. I loved this car. It was very pretty with all the wood and its style of design. It had a very nice, smooth ride to it. Well after I switched jobs I was not bringing home as much as I once was, so I had to let it go back to the bank. Well, let me tell you, my ego had a field day with this. All of a sudden I became less of a person. A total failure, because I couldn't afford something that was so nice. Even with all my training of the ego, my ego still has a mind of its own. Every time someone asked me where the Jag was, I became six inches tall. I even lied a few times because my ego just couldn't say, "Martin, you can't afford that car anymore." It took me a good time to get over this. How I did it was to separate myself from my ego. Once I was able to do that I could see that I am not a failure just because I don't have that Jag. I am the same person I was before I bought the Jag. OK, maybe I am not driving as nice of a car as I used to, but deep down I am still me. Was buying the Jag a mistake? No because I enjoyed owning it for the few short months that I did. When money is better I will just go out and get another one if I wish to at the time. By then I may find something else I like better. Once I remembered that the Jag was just a thing, not my standing in life, I began to feel better about myself. Like I have said all along in my book, I am not now nor ever will be immune to my ego, but by being aware of it, this will help me deal with my feelings about things. After losing the Jag, I'll be damned if I didn't just get up the next day and keep on living. The thing was gone but the love of my family and friends was still there. My ego told me that my successful life was over, but a hug from a friend reminded me that was not really true. Remember this: The love of friends and family is like the foundation of a building. Once you have that strong foundation it really doesn't matter how big or high you build; if an earthquake hits a house and brings it to the ground the foundation is still there to rebuild. If you spend so much of your life building the building and no time maintaining the foundation, the building will fall anyway. With the foundation strong you can have large or small breakdowns in your life but are able to rebuild it. You can rebuild that building as high or as "successful" as you want it to be. You can have the nicer car, bigger house, and more success in your career. Why, because your foundation is strong and YOU want it for yourself and the ones you love and care about.

Chapter 7

In this part of the book I would like to talk to you about the image you have of yourself. Everyone in life worries from time to time about what others think about him or her. They give very little thought about the image that they see for themselves. I have a new concept for everyone to try to swallow. You are what you think you are. What I mean is that you can be any kind of person you want to be by thinking you are. I know—"OK, I think I am a millionaire; where is all the money?" Well, there is a little more to it than just thinking it. Here is the formula for making whatever you think of yourself. Let's say that the problem is you wish you were more of an outgoing person. First you think you are a more popular and outgoing person. You "THINK" this thought for several weeks in a row so you can start to "BELIEVE" it. Then you do some action, like going out with your friends on Friday night, or meeting new friends. This would be the "DO" part of the steps. If you "DO" enough action you will "BECOME" the more outgoing person you wished that you were. Everything that you wish you could be is at your fingertips if you are willing to let yourself do it. In trying to achieve most of your goals in life you will be your own worst enemy most of the time. Oh, you will blame it on the world around you but it is you that will stand in your way most of the time.

One of the first steps in changing the image of you is learning to like yourself. You cannot have a bad image of yourself and like yourself at the same time. There are certain parts of ourselves that most of us do not like about ourselves. We all justify this by saying, well, that is just the way I am. Well you are that way because you believe you are that way. That makes you do the action that makes you become what you believe you are. Here is an example of what I mean: If you are an uptight person, first you must believe that you are an uptight person that creates the action in certain situations that you run across in life that make you react in an uptight way. When you act in the uptight way, you can justify it to yourself what you believe is true. Once you change your belief in yourself, it will cause you to react differently. The excuse of "I am that way" is just an excuse because you are that way because of the programming you have given yourself. Once you change the programming you can change the action. If you are able to change the action for a long enough period of time, you will be able to change your belief about yourself and then you magically become the new person. There is more than just thinking it. Here is the formula for making whatever you think of yourself a reality.

1. First you must think about what you want.
2. You must be able to believe what you want can become true.
3. You must take the action to make it become true.

Here it is stated in raw form:

1. Think.
2. Believe
3. Do.
4. Become.

It is really just that easy. Like I have stated before, not easy, just simple. If your mind can conceive an idea, you mind can achieve the idea. You know it is funny that the only person that can make a dream come true is the same person that will fight you the whole way. This person is you. You will find a lot of things in your life that could have happened, but you didn't wish to change your life to make it become a reality. There have been lots of times in my life where I could have really made a difference in my life and what did I do? Stop myself short by saying, "Martin, this is just a dream; it could never happen for you." I know, your next question is, "How did you stop yourself from doing this?" Well, I still do it, and always will. Remember, we all live in a negative world; it is very easy for each one of us to justify the negative. How you come out on top in this is to be aware of yourself and the negative thoughts that hold you back. This will be achieved by the self-talk I have talked about in earlier chapters. Getting to know why you react to new things the way you do will give you a good idea of why you have failed in the past. Sometimes, these negative thoughts will stop you from doing something that you would have failed at. But tell me this: which is worse, trying and failing or not trying at all? It is the times that we do not try that we really fail. And that is the only time we really fail. Trying new things is first a learning experience. That is a winning factor. It is in time of change that we grow; this is another winning factor. Learning what your limitations truly are is another winning factor. If you have done all these winning factors in the process of failing, that makes you a winner in many factors, and a loser at only one.

There is a factor of common sense in this. What I mean is you don't just kill someone because you envision yourself as a killer. Without selling yourself short you can learn the limits of yourself. This is a fine line; you may think you are giving it your all, but it will be the negative side of you telling you that you have done your best. It is when you have a good image of yourself that you can overcome the negative that is fed to you on a daily basis. OK, the next question is, how do I build a better image of myself. Well, the best way is to learn about yourself and the way you are versus the way you wish you are. If you find that you have shortcomings in some areas that you wish you were better at, then you have a game plan to work on. This is where you put into action the 4 set plans to change yourself. Well, did I lose you yet? OK, let's do an example saying that people never change. There is a lot of truth in that statement because as an observer of another person, if there is a quality about a person that we do not like, we will look for that quality in that person to repeat itself. As soon as we see that quality again, it will justify our belief that people do not change. This is a sad thing because that action of that person can change; with only an occasional repeat of the action we write it off as them not changing their person. Say, if a person is rude all the time. If a person that is rude all the time works on himself as being more polite, we have a belief in our head that this person is rude and when he is polite more often will not give credit for that person changing but will wait for him to be rude again to justify the fact that people never change. The worst part about all of this is we will not reinforce the new behavior but actually reinforce the old behavior in our actions and thoughts to him. This is one of the reasons why I always try to look for the positive in people. If you spend all you time looking for the positive in a person you will not be making light of the negative in that person. All people have good qualities as well as bad ones. We all tend to ignore the good qualities about a person and dwell on the bad ones. When we refer to that person to others we will either directly or indirectly transfer some of the bad qualities to a new person to justify the way we feel about them. If you are ever asked to describe a person to another, just point out the positive. If you relay the negative you will start the seed of negative in the new person as well. He will build on that for his opinion of the person. If you start the seed of positive they will build the positive until they experience the negative from that person to form their own opinion of the negative. Once they start to build on the negative of the person then it will change not only the way they picture that person but the way they react to them as well.

The sad part is that once they start to treat that person in that way, it will reinforce the bad attitude in that person. It is like a guy who is always cranky. People around him know he is always cranky and treat him that way. Him being treated special because he is cranky will most of the time just piss him off more. It is a never-ending circle. The same is true about all behavior patterns; if a behavior pattern is supported by others it will remain in effect. Well, once again you might ask, "Why are you talking about all this right in the section of changing the image of yourself?" Well, my answer to that is that change must come from one person; that is you. I know—"Martin, are you saying that I can change a person by changing myself?" Yes, it is true because of your interrupter. If you change the way you see a person that you deal with, then you will not reinforce the negative behavior; you will start reinforcing the their positive behavior. Once you start to take some of the energy out of their negative behavior you will not reinforce his behavior that he is trying to justify. This most of the time will not be enough to change that person, but it will be enough to change his attitude when he is dealing with you. Some people you will have to reprogram each time you see them. But by the time you are midway through your visit you will see the change in his attitude toward you. If you have exposure to this person every day or at least several times during a course of a week, you will find that it will be easier each time to reprogram his attitude when he is with you. By changing his attitude toward him he will feed you the positive input you need to keep a positive attitude. There are a lot of you that decide the image of yourself by the input you receive from others. By changing that input you change the output. This will make you feel better about yourself and improves your self-image. Now I don't want you to think this is the only factor. It is only a small factor when it comes down to it. The biggest factor is the thoughts you have about yourself and the picture you draw for yourself every day. If you think, you are. That is the general theory on changing your self-image. Now let's go through some practices you must start doing every day to improve it. This is the "DO" part of the equation. Start by finding something about yourself that you would like to change. The first two actions you must "DO" are thinking of what it is you wish to change and then thinking of times when you were weak in this area and what you could have done to be stronger. Then think of times you are strong in this area. No matter what the subject is there is a time in your life when you were strong in this area. Now that you have found the time you were strong, you can believe that you are able to be strong. By now, you are starting to say to yourself, "OK, I was strong this one time but the other thousands of times I wasn't." See, this is what I meant by the statement you are your own worst enemy. It is normal to have thoughts like these; it is your ego saying I am comfortable with this action and don't want to change. All you need to know is the fact that your ego is so used to the fact that you are weak in this area and will put ideas in your head to keep you at that level. It will take you to do different action than you normally would to make the new action happen. This will be uncomfortable for you at first. But after you repeat the action enough it will become the norm. Here is a good example of what I am talking about. I was finding myself having bad days all the time where everything that I did always went wrong. Well first I decided that I never again was going to have a bad day. Well, I proved myself wrong within a week. The reason I proved myself wrong was because I thought it but didn't believe it. Well, the next action in the 4 steps is believe. So every morning I got up and started telling myself that I was going to have a great day. Then I started an action of where everyone I ran into in a course of a day would say, "Have a nice day," and I would reply, "I always do." This started to change my life. At first my ego told me, "This is stupid, Martin; you sound like a dork." At times I almost had to choke it out of me, or I mumbled it. At this time I was fighting myself to "DO" this action. After a while of mumbling I forced myself to say it louder and mean it. I started looking forward to the next time I would get the chance to challenge myself to say it again. After a while I got to the point where I said it each time I was asked without mumbling it. This is when I started believing it. Well, after I started believing it, I started saying it without even thinking. Once I started believing it, I looked at my life and sure enough I wasn't having bad days anymore. By forcing myself to believe this, I did the action to justify by belief all day long that I was having a great day. Everything that I would do that day, good or bad, I really believed that my day was going great. Others around me would even comment, "How can you be having such a great day today? It is raining," or this or that is going wrong. Well some things might be going wrong, but I am happy to be alive and have so much to look forward to after work, and once this bad thing is taken care of, I am going to enjoy the rest of the day. You know the funny part about all of this is, at first, my co-workers wanted to see what they could do each moment of the day to see if they could make it bad for me. They didn't do this to try to ruin my good day, but to justify their bad one. Well once they saw that they couldn't ruin my day, their attitudes toward me changed. They didn't come to me with bad news, only good. Once you have decided you are having a bad day, you seek out a person that will help you justify that bad day. The last thing you want to find is a person that is having a great day. By the same token if that person is having a good day, they know to come to you and tell you about their great day. They come to you because they know you will justify their good day. What I am trying to say in all of this is that the believing is the most important factor in everything you want to do or become. Once you start to really believe, the "DO" part of it will become easier and the become part will just be there. In the become part of the 4 steps, that in itself does not require action. The think, believe, and do require action and from these actions you will become. What I really mean is you can't just become the way you wish you are. You can think, believe, and do; then you will become.

In this next section I would like to talk about setting and achieving goals. Goals are important for all of us to have; they give us a sense of direction and purpose. Well, you might say, "Martin, I have set some goals in the past, but never made them." I am going to tell you something you may not have thought about: You really did win in those goals. This statement about goals is very true: The only way you can really fail at your goals in life is to not set any. When you set a goal, you have bettered yourself, whether you achieve the goal or not. While it is important to try your best to achieve your goals it is not important whether you make them all the time or not. It is the journey towards achieving that will allow you to grow and make you a better person. By setting a goal this will give you a direction of action to make you a better person. Think of it like this: We get up in the morning and have breakfast. Why do we eat breakfast? It is because we are hungry. Well, we eat breakfast and around about noon we are hungry again. Long about night we are hungry again. It doesn't matter if we had breakfast or lunch; we are still hungry at the end of the day. Goals are like this; it doesn't matter if we fail or not in the big picture. We try again with that same goal or make a new goal. Now I am going to talk about some of the methods you can use to achieve a goal.

The Step Method of Achieving Goals...

In the step-by-step method of reaching a goal, you first state the objective of the goal.

This would be what you want to happen. Then you will list the things that have to happen before the goal can be reached. After you list the steps that must happen, you will then set up each step as a goal and work to make each step. I would set a date deadline for each of the steps. If you do not make the deadline just backdate the step for another short period. Then backdate each of the following steps as well. This method will help you to make the big goals. You will find that even a very hard-to-reach goal will be easier if you break it down into steps.

Written Goals: Short and Long Term

To have a goal you should write it down. When you write it put it into two groups. The first group should be short term. These should be easy-to-reach goals with planned reach dates. The other should be a long-term goal; these goals are bigger and harder to reach. If you are using the step method, you should put the end goal in the long term, and the steps into the short term. If you wish you could even make a medium term; this would be for goals that are really short term and you use the short term for weekly/monthly goals. Whichever system you use make sure you write them down. When they are on paper they are a something that is set versus in your head where they can be forgotten or ignored. When you have goals you will find yourself working to improve your life. It doesn't matter if we had breakfast or lunch; we are still hungry at the end of the day. Goals are like that.

Chapter 8
Raising Positive Kids

As a modern day parent our kids are growing up in a different world than we did. When I was a kid I spent most of my time playing with matchbox cars. Not my kids. This is the time of Nintendo and computers. All of my kids are computer kids. They spend as much time on the computer as I do. Mostly playing games but even playing computer games for kids is a good learning experience. It gets them used to computer controls and the keyboard. My youngest son has been on the computer since the age of two. He is very good with typing and has mastered Windows better than most adults I know. It is funny that when I get a new game for the computer I let my kids learn it first then take the time to show Dear Old Dad. My oldest has been on the computer since the age of five. At eleven years old he could write a letter on a word processor and spell check it and fax it. All of my kids make good grades in school; one of the reasons is the computer experience and the other is me. You might say that is pulling my own chain but it is true. When I was growing up it was a different kind of world; when we wanted to play we made up things. We did not have the graphic animation of Sega and Super Nintendo. Our graphics were made up by the imagination inside each one of us. Some might say that this made us more creative people and that our kids will not be. Well, I am glad to say that is not the way it is. My kids' imaginations are alive and working. As we used sticks for guns my kids use computers and even Nintendo for their source of creative outlets. If you do not think this is true, you have never sat down with your kids when they are trying to beat a level of a game. They learn each trick of the program and have to use that trick to beat the level. You know I have seen my sons come up with many creative ways to get past a bad guy in a video game. Creativity is creativity. It doesn't matter if it is from the stick, or the video game; they are just the tools, and the creative thought is still there. It is our job as parents to keep the creativity in our kids alive. We can do this by playing with our kids. Yes, you heard me right. I play with my kids when I get the time. I share in their interests and hobbies. I take the time to play computer games with them and share in their hobbies. My kids and I share quite a few interests. Computers being one of the interests.

Making friends with your kids—you can be a parent and friend to your children. I talk to my children all the time not as a parent but as their friends do, using the modern lingo and all. Some of you might think that will lose respect from your children, but respect is something that your kids have to give you, and being able to relate to them will give you the respect that most parents cannot get by being an uptight jerk. It is very important to open up the lines of communication with your kids. That is the only way to get to know them. As an example I will tell you about each one of my kids and the relationship I have with them. My oldest is my son David; his main interest is cars. He loves NASCAR and building models and sports cars. So when I am with him, we spend time building models together and talking NASCAR, and when we are riding I point out the hot sports cars.

My middle son, Chris, is into science, so he and I spend our time talking about physics and matter and antimatter. His knowledge of quantum physics is outstanding. My youngest is into cartoons and TV, so when we are together I sit and watch cartoons with him. You might say you don't know what your kids are interested in. Well that is exactly what I am saying. If you do not know, you should. Every kid has an interest in something. Some things may not be what you like; with little effort you should be able to find a way to enjoy what they enjoy. We all have the programming in us to raise our kids the way we were raised. I have heard out of parents' mouths over and over "That is the way my father raised me and I didn't turn out so bad." This is why some people have trouble being a parent. Like I have said earlier in my book, when we grow up it was in the "father knows best" era. Dad was lord of the manner, and when punishment came down it was when dad got home from work. Well, when this dad comes home from work, he talks to his kids about their problems, and instead of punishment, we talk about what could have been done to prevent the trouble in the first place. I want my kids to think of me as a counselor, not a judge issuing punishment. Don't get me wrong, I believe in punishment when it is necessary. But what you will find is that the necessity for punishment does not come when you have open lines of communication. Let's face it; the main reason for punishment is to let them know something bad happens when they mess up. Well, what I do is to point out all the bad things that could have happened, based on the action they had taken. I have seen over and over again parents that are quick to send a kid to the corner or rule with a belt or board have brats for kids. Why? Because they are putting all the attention on the negative behavior. The kid gets to know that if he/she does something wrong, BOOM, Mom or Daddy start to pay attention to them. So, when they want some parent attention, just do this. Well, my kids know if they want some attention, just talk to me. When I was married, I would come home some days and my wife would be at the top of her throat chewing out one of the kids. Then she gave them the "Wait till your father gets home" statement. Well, my kids are glad when Father gets home when she says that. I will get home and the guilty party will come to me and say, "Dad, I screwed up." Then he will tell me what he did wrong, and then he will tell me what he should have done instead. I will usually show a little disappointment in their action to show that I do care. Then I remind them that the next time they are in the same situation to keep in mind the solution they just gave me and then I change the subject and talk about the rest of the day. You might ask, "Is this what I should do with my kids?" I say yes, eventually. Take your time into easing this course of action into your kids. Here is the reason why: If your kids have been growing up with the knowledge that bad action gets attention, then if you just up and use this style of parenting they will just think that what they did wasn't bad enough to get attention and will try to top it. You will have to ease this style into effect. Why is this style so important?

Because I want my kids to do right, not because they know they will get an ass beating by Dad but because it is the right thing to do. Here is a good example about what I am talking about. I have a friend that is a single mom. During the course of every day, if she is not spanking her kids, she is threatening to do so. Well, when I am over to visit I will see the kids do things right in front of us to get their mom to come over and spank them. Well, one night a family emergency came up and I had to stay with the kids while she went away for a couple of hours. Before she left she said to the kids, "Martin will tell me if you guys do something wrong and I will spank you when I get home." Well, not wanting to disappoint Mom, as soon as she walked out the door they both went and did everything they could to insure they had that spanking when they got back. They started with small stuff at first and were confused when Martin didn't yell, so they tried some more advanced stuff. Well, in the middle of some of the most advanced things they could think of at the time, I asked them why they were doing that.

Of course I got the standard "I DON'T KNOW." Well I came up with one of the wittiest things at the time. I told them they must be doing it because they don't like me. I said, "If you liked me you wouldn't be doing things that hurt my feelings." They came over and hugged me and said they were sorry and started to pay attention to me, and played with me instead of trying to find things to get into trouble with. Well, after a while MOM came home, she asked me how the kids were and I looked at them, and they were looking at me, and I said that they were little angels. Their mom looked at them both and said, "I can't believe that," and one of the kids ratted out the other by saying well, he did this, this, and this. He said she did that, that, and that. Well, Mom decided that they should be spanked but she was going to let them off this time. Well, I stayed around for a little while to hear about the family emergency; the kids went back to doing things to piss her off. Everything was back to normal. Well, the next time I came over, the kids remembered that I want attention from them by not acting up and that was the way they were when Mom was out of the room. I took all the energy out of their negative behavior and made them think about my feelings and me. Did I change these kids' overall behavior? No, they still don't want to disappoint Mom, but when I am around they don't want to disappoint me. So, they don't act up. Is Mom doing wrong, well, that is in the eyes of the mother. She was most likely raised that way and thinks she has to be that way to be a good parent. That is something I would like to touch on now. The Good Parent Syndrome. What is a good parent? Is a good parent one who spanks their kids, doesn't spank their kids or grounds their kids? I don't want you to get the wrong idea. I am not against grounding your kids or spanking your kids, I just don't think it is necessary. The purpose of spanking and grounding is to make the kids realize that what they have done is wrong. Well, if you talk to them during a time when they are doing the wrong behavior, you can get that message across. One of the most important reasons is your kids don't have to hide or lie about things. My kids know if they go to Dad with something they have done wrong they can talk to me about the guilty feelings they have and not get the punishment from me. Most kids will punish themselves with guilt far worse than I could ever do. Just like you and I they will do far more beating on themselves than I could do. All kids have this in them; some just have it turned off. What I mean by that is they spend so much time in hot water with their parents that they just decide what the hell and do what they want. They have what I call a "nothing to lose" attitude. This is why we have so many teens in trouble. They have separated themselves from the family and have made family out of the other teens who have done the same. This is where gangs get started. They look for the comfort of someone who understands how they feel and after a while will even develop the rest of the group's ideas. This comes from having a low self-esteem. With no stable home life, it makes them feel that they are an outcast. They will hang with others that are outcast to feel they are a part of a group "family." That is why a lot of gangs are like "families." You will have a father figure and the rest are brothers, with some of them taking the older brother "leader" role. Now you might say, "Well, Martin, my son is in a gang, I have given him a good home life and he still hangs with the wrong crowd." Well, this might be true. I am not saying you're a "bad" parent; your son or daughter, for some reason, must feel separated from you. This could be something you are doing unknowingly or it could just be your child has this idea from inside of himself. Now you might ask what do I recommend that you do. Simple: no matter how deep your child is in I recommend that you STOP being a parent to this kid. YES, I said stop being a parent! You will have to start by being a friend to him. Stop for a moment and really think about which is more important, the "idea" of what we think a parent should be like, or the child who has separated himself, probably because of that same action. You know when I say stop being a parent this doesn't mean stop loving or caring for that child, it means stop yelling and getting pissed off at him.

Start trying to understand him. Talk to him about the things that interest him and tell him about what you went through as a teen. Note— do not turn this into a lesson speech, but tell him about times when you felt left out or lonely. This will help him more than a lesson speech because right now he feels you do not understand what he is going through. Right now, this kid feels like we were born parents and don't understand the stress of girls, school, friends, and parents on our asses all the time. He needs to know that you have "been there/done that" as the saying goes.

This approach might set off a time bomb. Remember, this kid is not used to talking about his feelings and may not want to or may totally unload on you. You will have to wait and see. If the child doesn't want to talk, keep at him until he opens up. If the kid unloads on you let him. Let him just get it all out. Then when he is done don't yell back but calmly talk to him about what he is saying. Remember you don't have to justify to your child the actions you have taken to try to be a good parent. You are doing what you think is right. You may have to admit that you could have handled some things better. There is nothing wrong with admitting you made mistakes with your child. Remember, there is not such thing as a perfect parent; we all are just trying to do our best. If a child sees that you are not always right and that you are also worried about screwing up as a parent this will help break down the wall that he has put between you and him. Something to keep in mind is that the only side of you this child has seen is the yelling and screaming.

If you stop doing that he might think you care even less; you will have to replace that with hugs and talking. You might be saying, "Yes, Martin, I yell and scream because I love them." You know that is true, I even know that is true, but the most important person doesn't know that is true. He thinks you do it just to fulfill you requirements as a parent or something dumb like that. You ask any kid why their parent is on their ass all the time; they will come back with the good old "I don't know." Even if they say because they care they will always add, "I wish they could find a better way." Well that better way is talking.

The best way to raise a positive kid is to look for the positive in your child.

Make sure to point out good qualities about your kids every moment you can.

We spend so much time jumping on their asses about the times they screw up just to overlook the times when they are doing well. As parents we have quite a bit to do with our kids' self esteem. It all starts at a very early age; you have all heard the saying the terrible twos. As parents we have this image of what the terrible twos are like so we look for our child's behavior to justify what we think the terrible twos are like. I am guilty of this myself. I looked for the terrible twos in all my children. And guess what, I found it. That is what I am talking about. I have had many parents say to me, "You think the terrible twos are bad, wait till they get to be a teenager." Well, I want you to know I have a teenager, and he loves his music and hanging with this friends and forgetting to tell me where he is from time to time. But I do not point out these qualities to him. I remind him of all the times he is responsible and let him enjoy his music. I am lucky in one way: he likes county music, not rap. But even if rap was his music of choice then I would sit down and listen to it with him from time to time. Why, because teens are programmed to be rebels. They are told by their friends and by other adults that if a parent doesn't like something then it must be cool. Well, once you take the rebel out of a rebellious teen all you have left is a teen. A teen that knows what he likes, not a teen that likes something because you don't like it. Now don't get me wrong, you don't have to listen to his music all the time, just when you are with him, devote one of the car radio buttons to him. The way I see it I would rather suffer through a little rap or hard rock than suffer through the teen that is rebellious. Now don't get me wrong, I am not saying give the teen his way all the time. There are certain times when he will want to do something and you will have to say no. But by giving in on what you can give in on, then even the times when you have to say no, it will go over better. When you say no to a teen don't just say no, tell them why; they will come up with a hundred comebacks why your "why" is not good enough. You know one of my favorites responses to that is "Good try, but you still can't go." You know this is the funny part. If your teen wants to do something that you know he is going to get himself in trouble, and you say no, well if everything turns out OK for the teen that went you are the bad guy, but if the teens get into trouble and your son didn't go, in the back of his head he will be glad you said NO. A very important factor in all of this is talking to your teen all the time. If you can be one of the programming factors in your teen's life then it will help when you have to say NO. Remember bitching him out or yelling at him all the time is not the same as just talking to him. If you yell too much he will just tune you out of his life and the programming will come from the other kids who had tuned out their parents as well.

By talking to your teen as one of the kids would, you can be part of the programming instead of one of the things your teen has programmed out. My teen's friends when they come over treat me as one of the boys and even talk to me about girls, family problems and more. I like this. I don't want to be a "PARENT" at these times, I want to be a friend that my teen or his friends can talk to about things. Why, because part of the programming my son takes in is from these kids, so if I can help their programming I am helping my son's programming as well. This doesn't mean that I hang out with them all the time; that would be too geeky even for me. I let them have time to themselves but I do let them hang with my teen and me when we are going to do something together. Do you know I actually like a lot of my son's friends. He has good taste when it comes to picking out friends. I would like to think that I had something to do with that. I hope that he has learned from my choice of friends and how thoughtful I am as far as helping them out and being there with an open ear when they need someone to talk to. I see that he treats a lot of his friends in the same manner I treat my friends. If you can develop the relationship with your kid and the friends of your kids you will be more a part of their life and will be able to have more effective control on your child's behavior than if you are the traditional parent. The traditional parent is the one that the kids blow off because as a kid they are expected to. This is where role-playing in a family tends to take over. See as a parent I am supposed to act a "certain" way, and as a kid, they are supposed to act a "certain" way. Well, I remind you of what I said before. It is more important to have a good relationship with your child than the "traditional" relationship with your child. I don't want to be the parent that my child blows off and thinks that I am just on his case all the time for the hell of it. You can remain the good parent and say no to your kids when you have to. The think to change is your attitude toward them. Remind them all the time of their good points and help them with the things they are weak in. This is what I have done with my kids and they are different acting kids than most. My kids not only love me, they actually like me as well.

Chapter 9
You Are a Complete Person

In this chapter I would like to talk to you about being a complete person. Each one of us is divided into many different parts. Listed below are some of the different parts of ourselves we all must deal with.

Parts of the complete person

1. Ego
2. Inner Self
3. Pride
4. Humility
5. Boldness
6. Bashfulness
7. Sincerity
8. Non Sincerity
9. Anger
10. Happiness
11. Joy
12. Depression

These are just some of the things that we all have within us to make us the complete person that we are. Some of these traits are more in control of you than other traits. This is something that we must all deal with; the big question that needs to be answered is who is in control of this part of you. This is where you can make a big difference in your life by taking control of each one of these parts of yourself. Here is an example of what I am talking about. A person gets mad at another person and shoots him.

Well, that means that anger took control of him, instead of him controlling the anger.

If a person is suffering from depression that means depression is in control of him.

Now I want to go on record by saying now, to take control of a part of you does not mean eliminating this part. We all need those parts of us to be a complete person. It is OK to get angry, it is OK to be depressed, as long as you are in control. Now, you might ask OK, Martin how do I take control. This is done through self-talk. When you are angry, say to yourself OK I am angry that is OK. Then ask yourself why am I angry. Then ask yourself OK why does that anger me? Once you come to the second question, you start to get to know yourself a little better. You can do this for all the sides of you good and bad. This will help you to understand yourself.

When you are happy recognize that you are happy, ask yourself why am I happy. Then ask yourself why does this make me happy. It is very important to find out the why's for two reasons. If it is something like anger, you will find out more about yourself and things to avoid making you angry. If it is something like happiness you can find out what makes you happy and repeat this when you want to be happy again. Understanding yourself will give you a better edge in being a better complete person.

You know there are a lot of people out there that try to separate their business life from their personal life. I have some earth-shattering news for them, they really can't achieve this. You are a complete person, not a divided person, that is why a businessman can be happy or pissed off at his place of work. It is getting to know yourself that makes a difference. If you are a person that tries to show no emotion at work, you might find yourself with a short temper at home. This would be the complete part of yourself trying to equal itself out. If something happens at work to anger you it is OK, but you don't have to let the anger at work control you, you can control it. Use the self-talk method and find the real reason that you are angry and base your action on the reason not the anger. Once you start to do this you will find that you can deal with work stress a lot better. You will not bottle it up to unload on the family at home. Just the opposite is true as well, if something is going on in your personal life then you may be short with people you know at work. One thing to keep in mind, the only difference in the angry guy that goes out and shoots someone and an angry guy that yells at someone is the degree of control over the anger. Both are a response based on the emotion anger, not an action based on why we are angry. Once you come down to the reason why we are angry then we can use that motivation of the feeling of being angry to our advantage. Did I lose you on that statement; OK here is a common example. You do a lot of work on a project; once it is done you turn it into your boss and he turns it over to his boss and gets all the credit. OK, this makes you angry, this is OK, you can now ask yourself why am I angry, well that is an easy one. I did the work and he got the credit. Next ask yourself what you want out of this, Well, more credit for work you have done. Next is the action part, you can go to your boss and tell him that you are disappointed that you did to receive the credit for your part of the project. See if he were a good boss he would not have taken the credit for it himself, but given the credit to you in the first place.

If he failed in that responsibility then he should be reminded that he failed in that responsibility. You don't need to tell him this but if he ever fails in that responsibility again, that you should go to his boss and let him know you did all the work. You can do this not by "ratting" him out, but by saying to his boss, I personally did all the research for this project and if you need any further details feel free to ask.

This way you are letting the big boss know who really did the work, and show team effort. Keep in mind that interoffice politics are an unfortunate reality. If you do not play the game sometimes, they will just keep skipping your turn.

I would like to take a moment at this time to talk about interoffice politics. All Interoffice politics is a big ego game, who will get the promotion, raise or credit for work done. Unfortunately sometimes it is not who deserves the promotion that gets it, it is the one best at playing the game. To me this is a very sad fact about corporate America, but never the less it is a reality. You must learn the game to get ahead. The funny part about it I can't tell you how to learn the game, because it differs from company to company. I can tell you about the basic factors in the game. The number one fact is ego. What you have is a group of egos working and competing with each other. See the ego is where most of your self-confidence comes from. If you can learn to develop your self-confidence without letting your ego run amuck, you will be better at the game. How many times have you seen an ego control ass that gets a promotion. It happens all the time, why, because even though his ego is in control, he will have a higher sense of self-confidence. It is when you can show that higher sense of self-confidence that you begin to go up in corporate America. A lot of times a boss who has good people under him will tend to take credit for everything that they have done. Why, because he knows that without the team's work he is nothing special, just another timecard in the slot. To play the game he knows that it is him that has to get all the credit in order to be able to take his turn. I know what you are thinking about now, Martin, I can't believe you are telling me after all your teaching in previous chapters to play this ego game. Well, I have news for you; you are going to be in this game, one way or another, either as a player or as a victim. So, you might as well be a player, if you want that promotion. If you want to go to work and just collect your paycheck on Friday, you will most likely be better off, in my opinion.

It is OK to do that, if you wish to advance you will have to play the game. It is OK, to do that as well. Just keep in mind that your self-esteem is what gets you that promotion not the ego.

I would like to take a moment to talk about Job Stress. I have a statement to say that you are not going to believe at first. The statement is this: There is no such thing as a Stressful Job! ! ! I know, what you are thinking, Martin you are full of Buffalo Bagels. OK, maybe so, but the statement is still true.

To see this you need to know what stress really is, it is self-induced pressure that we put on ourselves. You can have a very active job, like running a store, a department, or any position where lots is going on all the time. This is just having an active job. The stress comes from the pressure we put on ourselves to do the job better. Do you know that at least 50% of all job stress is caused by factors that we have no control over. That 50% is an understatement for most of us. If you are in a upper-level management position it is most likely because your personal work habits are under control. Meaning that the things you do have control over are under control, otherwise you would not be keeping the job you have. It is the factors that you are responsible for but don't have control over what causes stress. I know, OK Martin I can see what you mean but what can I do about things that I don't have control over. Well, there are several things you can do, first and most important is realize that even though you are responsible for this area, you are not responsible for the actions of others. When these things happen, you need to stop playing The "IF" game, meaning maybe IF I had done this, it would have turned out differently. You need to self talk some more, and first find out what is the real problem. Once you find the real problem, don't focus on the stress but focus on the problem itself; this will give you a sense of control over the problem factor. This action might include several different factors, maybe talking to a weak link in your department, or even having to let go of that weak link, if the pattern does not stop. If stress factor is coming from the upper levels of management from you, this is the time to put the your ego in your back pocket and go to your boss, after you have found the reason for the problem and ask some advice from him. Remember, he/she is putting pressure on you to get a certain response or action that they feel should be made. Find out what they want and explain what the real factors are and together come up with a solution, then act on that solution. Keep in mind that as upper management if they are going to provide the pressure they should also be willing to provide the solution. If they can't come up with a solution once you have presented the true problem to them, then most likely they are putting unwarranted pressure on you. Now, keep in mind that this is not always true, they may not have an answer to your problem, but they don't have any right to complain once you have tried to solve the problem yourself. They should be reminded when they put pressure on you that they had the chance to get the kind of results they wanted.

This is not showing weakness, this is giving them a chance to be a part of your responsibilities. As your boss then is responsible for your actions. So, by taking your solution to them it gives them a chance to put in their input. There is a chance that your boss will do a protect my ass PMA on you. Meaning that even if you follow his advice he will turn it around to say, something like that is not what I meant, if his plan backfires. If your boss has done this to you in the past get what is suggested in writing with a message and reply form. See unlike you he might have a problem in admitting he was wrong.

In this next section, I would like to talk about finding the good in other people.

Even though I have spent a little time on this in previous chapters, I think that it will not hurt to spend some more time on it. Getting along with all the people in this world helps us to learn more about ourselves. There is good in all people, some have been shit on so many times that it is hard to find it in some. But, when you spend your time looking for the good in a person and then pulling it out of them when they are with you it will make a difference in that person's life.

If a person is rude, most of the time to others, you can find out about that person and indirectly point out his rudeness to others. I know, Martin are you trying to tell me that I can change another person. NO, but you can change his attitude when he is around you. This is how, by example. When you are with this person in public places, take time to show how you are nice to them, even over do it a little. This person will not respond at first most likely, his rudeness is too deep.

But with enough exposure to you he will start to see the kind of reaction and result you get from people versus his reaction and result he gets from people.

I have a friend who is a real S.O.B. When he spends time away from me I can tell, we will go some place he will resort back to his old habits of being rude, until I show him again how to act again. I don't tell him direct, I show by example how to be nice to others. Another way to deal with this kind of person is to point out his good side all the time. This kind of person usually acts this way to get attention. He was taught as a kid, that acting in a rude way gets him attention. Whether it is

Negative or Positive attention doesn't matter, just the fact that it is attention. You can provide the attention that they need by reinforcing their positive behavior.

In this section of the book I would like to talk to you about the Art of Giving.

In today's world we have all learned through the school of hard knocks that the only person you can really depend on is ourselves. This is a very important lesson to learn because it makes us stronger people. Since everyone is looking out for themselves in the world, if we do not learn to look out for ourselves then we will be left out of life. After you is comfortable looking after yourself then it is time to go an extra step. This extra step is to reteach the world that we are all in this big world together. We need each other to survive. Most of us have forgotten this lesson because we are too busy looking out for #1. I know, Martin are you telling me that you want me to reteach an entire world. No, just reteach your little corner of the world. Give some time to you family, friends, and even total strangers. Time and friendship is the one thing that all of us have, that we can share. If a friend needs an ear, spare it for them. If a friend needs some help, help them. I am not saying money, money will make them dependent on you and others to survive. Just give them time, friends, and a helping hand with things that are important to them. This is time well spent even if that friend does not return the time to you. I am not saying do things for people that never return a favor. But you will have to make the first couple of times like a leap of faith.

Chapter 10
Managing Your Ego

In this book I have spent a lot of time talking about your ego. Once you start to get your ego under control, you will start to grow in a new awareness of yourself. You will start to get to know yourself better and be able to handle more in life. You will be able to understand some of the things that get you upset and why.

You will be able to think things out before you make decisions, and make a decision based on the facts. You will start to base you decisions on responding instead of reacting. The new you will not get upset over every little thing in life, he/she will know that some things are not worth getting upset over. Each one of us plays an important part of the world around us. Each person we deal with during the course of a day deals with hundreds more people during the course of their day. Even more is that each person they deal with deals with hundreds more each day. Have you had days when you run across a rude person, that really pissed you off and then you interact with others and some of this bad seed will rub off on them too. This chain reaction can happen for the good as well. If you are nice to everyone you meet, then that person will respond by being nice to others after a while of reprogramming.

Remember our minds are like computers in a way, when bad programming comes in bad programming will come out. When good programming goes in the good programming comes out.

I would like to talk about my reality. What I mean by this is what the world would be like if we all would follow the teaching from this book. This would be a world that everyone is in control of their own egos, instead of their egos controlling them. As you meet new people they would automatically become you new friend, you would not have any prejudgment about them, you would be able to accept them for what they are because they would be themselves. Dating would be far easier, if every girl or guy you met just acted like himself/herself instead of a front. The person you date would be the kind of person you marry. Guys wouldn't look for the hot looking girls only, his ego requires it, it would pick a girl that he likes because she has the same interest that he does, no matter what she looked like. The same is true for girls, she wouldn't really care what the guy looks like too much, more importantly what interests does he have. Marriages would last because you would be able to talk to your mate as you would your friends, because your mate would not react to what you say, he would respond with action to make you happier. Also, with his/her ego under control would not feel the need to have extra marital affairs. There also would not be any more wars, because one religion would not be bothered by the way another religion felt. There would not be racial hatred toward others, we would be able to accept each person based on their qualities, not the color of their skins.

It is the ego that tells us one color of skin is better than another. In my reality I would do away with money, this is an ego-driven item if I ever saw one. Just think, if you worked 40 hours to help manufacture a consumable item, and have proof that you worked the 40 hours, you can just go to the store and get the food you need for the week. You could have a house, car, everything you need in life, free. Basically that is what we are doing now, but they put in that money control factor. This is something to think about, it is not how hard you work that gets you money, it is your status. Here is an example, who physically works harder the corporate C.E.O. or the line worker over the machine all day. That is easy, the machine worker, which makes more money, the C.E.O. You know what the funny part about this is the C.E.O. will make 3 or 4 times the wage the line worker will per year. Without money, the company would get the raw materials it needs to make the product free. The worker would come to work because he is provided with food and housing and transportation. The C.E.O. would have to come to work just for the same reasons. The way things are now, the factory worker does most of the labor, just to barely put food on the table and make his monthly bills. The C.E.O. does less labor and enjoys the finer things in life. Just think a corporation would have given a promotion to another person that has the personal skills to do the job. If this person does not have the training, it will be his fault because it will not cost a dime to get yourself more education.

Just think, there would not be unemployment because companies would not pay wages. They would employ as many workers as needed to provide enough product for others to have. We are all doing this now, just the money control factor keeps the middle and lower class from enjoying everything they wish to have. Of course in my reality we will not need big fancy houses, just good ones that have the proper amount of room for your family. If you want a sports car, or fancy car that will be what you get. The manufacturers will have to produce them instead of the compact cars. You will get the kind of car you want, not because of status, anyone can have that same car, but because it is what you like. You can hang on to that car for a set amount of time, and trade it in. Of course if something goes wrong with the car mechanics work for free too, so you can just get it fixed.

You might ask, OK if this would be the way the world is, then what would keep everyone from owning a mansion. Well, first of all, without an ego, we would not need a mansion, just a house with enough room for your family and possessions.

If your house became too small you would just request a bigger one or hire a free contractor to expand the one you have. Now don't get me wrong I know this reality will never be but it is nice to think about. Maybe the money part of my reality can not be, but the part about dating and dealing with others can. When I was single, I have made a promise to myself not to act a certain way just to get a girl. Even though I know what kind of attitude attracts women. I am going to act like myself, that way when I find a girl that likes me she will be buying the whole package, not just the pretty wrapper. Too many times I see guys who buy flowers, sweet talk, and shower affection. Once he is with her for a while then he will not do these things. Well what does the girl think? First she thinks that his love for her is fading away, which may not be true. It may even be getting stronger, but you are not doing the little extras to show her how you feel. This is a sad but true fact, your love will grow stronger over time, but you will not express it in the ways you did when you first met. Love becomes an involuntary function, like breathing, if you don't breathe you will die, but you don't spend time thinking about it. Well love is the same way, if you don't take time to think about loving your mate the love will die. My advice to you is, take a little time each day and show the one you love, that you do love them. It might be as simple as a hug, or taking you mate out to dinner, just you and her. Talk to her/him about your life and when they talk to you about theirs listen.

Believe it or not, they are not just talking to themselves, they are talking for you to listen. It is a small thing to do, but some of us get into a pattern with our mates and don't know why we keep having problems with everyone we come across. Spend some time with others, we all get caught up in our own little worlds, we sometimes forget that there are other people on this planet with us. You know sometimes I am in a traffic jam looking around at the cars in front of me and around me and have to remind myself, in each one of the cars is a person. Each person, is in this traffic jam at the same time I am. Each person has his/her own world, they are on their way somewhere or going home from somewhere, I am just a few feet from this person in infinite size of the universe, and I may look over to them and they turn their heads from me. Like I wasn't even there. There have been many times in traffic jams, I would look over and smile at someone or wave to them. Yes, they would turn their head and think I am nuts, but some will smile back or wave back. I really don't have to know a person to be friendly with them. It is not a requirement for me, the person that I smiled at might be having a bad day and need someone to smile at them. Have you ever been sitting at a light and some cute girl/guy smiles at you. That will make your day, this has happened to me, I have had a bad day at work, feeling a little blue, and just a smile from a "stranger" will pick up my spirits. The funny part is even if this person I smile at thinks that I am crazy she will get a good chuckle out of it, and brighten her day as well. We all need to add a little sunshine to everyone every day this is the only way we will overcome all the negativity in this WORLD…

Chapter 11
Forever Is About Six Months Long

Hi, everyone, welcome to my second part of my book. I hope you are enjoying it. I wrote this book over a period of several years; in this time it has seen many changes in my life including the separation of my second wife and myself. After I separated from my second wife I really didn't date anyone for about a year. Then I started dating again until I meet someone I thought was the one. This is what I experienced with her and the valuable lesson I learned about my feelings. I changed my job and became self-employed, or self-unemployed as I call it. During self-employment I met a girl that I fell in love with. We only dated a short time and we got engaged and she moved in with me. I had a small apartment at the time and we looked around and found a nice house to move into. I spent every day of my relationship talking to her about our happiness and love for each other. I spent every night caressing her and holding her in my arms. Things were really good. She talked to me all the time about how much she loved me and I loved her and how every moment away from each other seem like an eternity. My business was doing really well and we had no money problems. This continued for months and we spent every day sharing the events and love we had for each other looking forward to the day when I could marry her and she could marry me. We set the date for Valentines, providing that her divorce was final. Now I don't want you to get me wrong, when I met her she was still legally married but separated from him. At the time I met her she was seeing a guy and things were not going well, according to her and she left him to move in with me. When she did this my friends cautioned me, and I thought about it as well that she just up and left this guy for me. I figured the reason why was because she fell in love with me and wanted to spend the rest of her life with me instead of him.

About the fourth month we were together, my business took a drastic turn for the worse. I made good money per hour but every week I worked less and less hours. At first she was very supportive, and even though money got tight, we were close. After the fifth month things got seriously worse. I decided it was time for me to look for a job. With my background of accounting and computers I thought it would be easy for me to get employment. But I had a big factor against me, I had college but I didn't have a degree. It took me almost two months to get an accounting job through a temporary agency. I got the job and worked it two weeks and they decided to go with a secretary position for the job for less money. Since my secretary skill was low I was called off the job. This is when things started to look bad we fell behind in our bills and things got tough. During this time at first my girlfriend was very supportive. Soon I decided to take any job, but because of my higher salaries and experience I found that most factories figured if they gave me a job I would quit for a position I was more qualified to do. Things really got bad, we made arrangements with the landlord to keep him from kicking us out. At the end my girlfriend started pulling away from me. I went out every day to look for work, and after a while, she stopped talking to me. Every day, I would see a little more slip away. I did everything in my power to show her that it was going to be OK, even though things looked bad. It was a couple weeks before Valentines that she started working longer hours. I not having a job, would do housework and when she got home got my attention and affection. But I started to notice that affection was only going one way. She would tell me she still loved me and wait till I said it back. I noticed then that her stories of when she was getting off and when she would get home would be different. She would come home to me and make love to me, then go back to not being affectionate. One week before Valentines she had to work over and didn't know what time she was going to get off. Well I woke up early that morning and she wasn't home yet. I called her work and they said she got off work at 11:00. Well, sometime around

10:00 am she shows up, she said that she worked a different area and they didn't know she was still there. I knew then the truth. I accepted her story and during the course of one week she had a couple hours every day where she would work over and on her day off she said she needed to go for a walk. It was the evening before Valentines that she came home from work crying that she needed some time to herself and went with her brother to spend the night making me kiss her good-bye before she left. The next morning she shows up and tells me she is moving out and got her own place. She got her own apartment the day she got paid and moved in the guy she had met at work. She had been seeing him for four weeks and only spent the two nights with him. This was Valentines Day the day we were going to get married. She left me with no food or money. The same day I finally landed a job. You might say well, can you blame her you were not working and she was looking out for herself. The fact is that within a period of one month she went from loving me forever, to cheating on me, to moving in with him. Now did she really love me? Some of you might say yes, but things got too bad and she went to someone else. When I first met her she didn't have a job and I supported us both, granted I was making good money but the fact is that I was out there working she was job hunting and it didn't matter. But turn the tables around and all of a sudden to most of you I had it coming.

When a family member why she left me asked my girlfriend her response was my boyfriend is working Martin is not. Where did everything go wrong, it was with my girlfriend?

Oh sure Martin blame it on her. See, I couldn't help the fact that I couldn't get employment, I was looking every day. When I met her she was not working, I didn't love her any less. My love for her was a true one that didn't have the price tag on it. Then the question was why did she give up on me so fast. The answer is love. When you love someone you have to put your faith in them and when times get tough you hold each other a little tighter. Look at any good long marriages, during some time in most marriages you will find a time when they had hard times. The couple stuck it out together and got through the hard times. That is what love is about. In these modern times it is an underlined rule that to survive you got to look out for number one. In a good marriage your number one cannot be yourself, but must be the one that you love. Remember this and you will see what I mean. If things got so bad that we had to give up our house, our cars, and any other material things, it is OK. Material things can be gotten again. If you give up your love for another to save those material things then what do you have left? All the material things, but not the most important the love of your mate. I would have given up everything I owned my clothes off my back, everything for her. She put a price tag on what she would give up for me. After I got my job, everything would have been OK. Bills got paid, and we would still have each other. She left me for another guy, but when it come down to it again she will sell out him to keep what she has now.

Dealing with her leaving me was very hard on me. I didn't eat, sleep or feel like doing anything for about a month. Will I ever get over her? Yes and no. Yes, after a while the pain will go away, but in my mind we were going to be together forever and I have a big void in my life. I was feeling pretty down about ever finding someone that is for me. Then one night at the local bar I ran across the girl of my dreams. She was smart, believed in forever love and we talked from the minute I sat down till closing time. She was living with another guy and was having troubles with him. I said good night, and it didn't go any further than that. But that gave me the hope that I will find someone else that feels about love the way I do.

Chapter 12
What Is Love?

I thought I would devote a chapter of this book explaining what love really is. OK I know what you are thinking, Martin what makes you such an expert on love, and your girlfriend left you for another guy. Well to respond to that question I must use an old saying that applies. It takes two to Tango. The one you are with has to love you as much as you love them or it will not work. See in this modern world we get taught from an early age to look out for number one. You really can't survive in this world if you don't look out for yourself. Everyone else is looking out for themselves and if you don't look out for you, then you will be swallowed up by everyone else. This statement is a hard reality about life in the modern world. Back in the past we spent more time looking out for our neighbors and others that live around us. Times were harder and sometimes just putting food on the table was hard for most families. So if you had a good harvest, you gave a little to the guy next door, and he did the same for you when times were better for him. Now in the modern world where we are looking out for number one, we have all these people that are getting swallowed up by everyone else's greediness and that is why you have homeless and poverty.

This is where love comes in. When you are able to put aside the needs of yourself, to put someone before yourself. The best example of this I can find is my shoe theory. If you are a parent and you have $ 30.00 left to your name and you and your child need new shoes. Who gets the new shoes, your child does. Why, because their needs are more important than yours. You could just as easy say to yourself, well all they do is play in them and go to school, I am out working all day in these holey shoes and need to get me a pair, they can wait. But, as parents we don't do things like that, we will live with the holes in our shoes, and buy them for the child, even if the child's shoes are less damaged than yours. This is love. Once the child has the new shoes then we will think about ourselves the next paycheck and get ours. You should have the same kind of love for you mate. If you are with someone you really love, your needs come second to his or hers. Do you know why? Because their needs come second to you. This is what love is; putting a person needs and wants before you. It has nothing to do with sex, kissing, hugs and other forms of what people think love really is. Not that these things aren't important, they are part of showing the person you love that you love them. But they are all just a part of love, not love itself. If you are the kind of person that comes home from work gives your mate a kiss and goes into the living room and plops in front of the tube for the rest of the evening then you are not really showing the love for your mate.

I have heard it said a hundred times; love is spelled T I M E. When my girlfriend came home from work, the first thing I always did was go into the kitchen put on a pot of coffee and sit with her and visit, hearing about her day at work and anything else she wanted to talk about. This was fun for me; it let me be a part of her life even when she was away from me. I would give up an hour or two every night of TV, to spend time with the person I love. It is not a big sacrifice. After she was done then I would go and watch some TV, and most of the time she would come in and watch with me. If she had stuff she wanted to get done instead, I went and watched by myself. But the important point of this is the time I spent with her. Granted you can overkill this idea, some people need some time to themselves. You will know when it is OK to go into the other room.

If you are with someone and are not doing this you should. But, be careful at first you might throw her/him for a loop. They are used to you not spending time with them and may reject it at first. If they do tell them what you are doing and that you love them and want to. I have seen so many times a couple together that he says I have tried talking with her and she won't with me, and turn around and find that the girl is saying the same thing. This type of relationship is common; it usually comes from bad timing. If your mate comes to you in the middle of a movie and wants to talk, or you go to her while she is busy doing things and want to talk, she will say she is right in the middle of this and will not really want to talk. Well that is where setting a pattern of visiting is necessary. When you set the time to the side every night, it will not build up. Use this time you have set aside, to talk about everything don't hold back. That is were most marriages fail is lack of communication. You should be able to tell your mate anything. If you have something you can't tell her/him then you must likely should not be doing it in the first place. Trust me; if you don't talk to your mate and you start spending time with them you can most likely expect an avalanche at first.

They will spend the first couple times quiet, because they are not used to this. Then you will get years of built up problems that you have not been facing about each other. Then you will go to the place where you can talk without bitching and become closer. Here are some of the phases, you might come across and how to deal with it.

Nothing to Say to Each Other

You would think, here is a married couple they are together all the time and can't even talk to each other. This marriage is doomed. Not really the main reason you can't talk to each other is not that you have nothing in common it is that you are not used to talking with each other. It will be awkward talking at first, both of you will have to come up with things to talk about. The best thing is feelings, I know for some guys it is hard to talk about your feelings. For some reason we think that being male you don't talk about the way you feel about things. She will never know how you really feel about her and your life together unless you tell her.

She can guess, but most of the time I have seen that she really doesn't know. She may think that because you don't talk to her or spend time romancing her anymore that you don't love her anymore, when just the opposite is true. You can find things in common to talk about, talk about the kids, talk about something that interests her. Talk about her work, the house, vacation plans, day to day living, anything you can think of at first, see after a while, just talking will come natural, and you won't need to find things to talk about, you will have plenty to tell her. It is just hard at first, don't give up it is too important.

Bitching Sessions
Don't be surprised if some of your talking turns into a bitching session. For one thing all these years together you have been talking at each other but not to each other. Now that your mate has an open ear, they might use the open ear to unload everything you have done wrong since they have known you. This is long overdue, so let them have her/his moment, don't lose your temper just sit and take it. This is the way they feel about things and you need to listen, not argue.

You need to know just how they feel about things, once they are done with their unloading pick up the pieces. What I mean by that is use a little understanding put yourself in their shoes for a minute and see why they are feeling that way. It could take little effort on your part to change some habits or ways of doing things that upset them. Granted, some things you can't change, but if you love this person and they are unhappy about something, then do your best to fix it. Some things can't be fixed, that is where you have to decide whether or not you can live with it. Sometimes you will find that some people do not want the problem fixed, they just want to bitch about it. Well, that is where you just sit and take it. This problem must be important to them if it is on their mind and they need someone to express their feelings about it to. You can be understanding and let them go. Help them if you can in dealing with the problem, by offering an idea or thought on how they can handle it. You can also help them find some peace with the matter by talking it out. If they complain about something, ask them why does this bother them, and then ask why does that make them mad. This is when you come down to the true feelings on why things upset you. Reading the first part of my book you would have known this already (hehe…). It is one of the ways I talk about getting to know yourself and self talk. But anyway, if you find out the true reason why something bothers your mate, then you can deal with the root problem instead of the bitching it is boxed in.

Keeping the Talking Alive

Once you get into the habit of setting some time to the side to talk to your mate every day, you might find yourself, slipping back to not talking again. You will have to watch this. It is easy to slip back into old habits and before you know it you will be back to not talking. We all have busy schedules, between working and house work and everything it is not easy to take the time sometimes but you have to; the future of your relationship depends on it. You know my grandparents stayed married till the day my grand father died. Every time I was over when I was a kid they would gripe at each other. That is the way they communicated. He did his own thing all day she did hers but they didn't lose that communication, they use the form of griping at each other to express it, but they always knew how the other felt about something. That is what is important, the communication.

Knowing your mate and how they feel about things in their life is a way of sharing life together. When you are married, you are no longer two separate people living together, but one couple sharing your lives together. Sharing your feelings of love for each other, anger for each other, disappointment for each other, everything. Once you have this, there will be little that will come between you. If you can talk to your mate about anything, they stop being your mate/husband/wife or whatever and start becoming your best friend. This is the goal of talking to not only have a mate, but to become friends.

I will talk more about this on my section on being friends with your mate. I just wanted to touch on it now because communication is the biggest key to a happy marriage. Next I would like to talk about showing affection. When you first meet a girl, we all are very romantic at first. There is lots of kissing and hugging holding hands, and other forms of affection. Well after a while that fades, it is only natural. This is where you have to on a daily basis, remind yourself just how much this person means to you. We all fall into a pattern of taking a person for granted, when they are there every day. Just like taking the time to talk, you need to take the time to be affectionate. You need to just hold them in your arms more often, kiss them more often, and hug them more often. I have a confession to make right now, this is one of the areas that I fell short in as far as my girlfriend. I got to a point where I didn't kiss her as often as I should, or when I did it was a short kiss. I walked out the door a couple of times having something else on my mind and didn't kiss her good-bye. Is this why she left me, no, not the only reason but it was part of the reason I am sure. I will talk about the main reason she left later in this book. This is something I am going to have to work on with my next girlfriend. Making sure that I take the time to be more romantic with her. Part of the reason I lost it a little, is because my affection toward the end became a one way street. Me giving and her taking. See when we first got together, she spent a lot of time with me in my arms every night. After we were together for a while I noticed her wanting to spend less and less time cuddling with me. She did this for her own reasons that I will talk about later, but my affection was not motivated toward the end to always give, give, give and not receive.

If you try this with your mate and they at first don't respond don't give up. They are used to things the old way, they are used to you pecking them on the cheek good night and you not hugging and holding them. It will take time at first to get used to it. I want to give you some ideas on keeping the passion alive.

Keeping the Passion Alive

This is very important to do. When you first meet someone you have the hots for them very bad. There is more sex, more kissing, and more affection. After a while of being together you will lose some of this. Not that you don't feel it, you just don't show it as often. This is where you can make some big changes in your life. You can make the heat again, by turning up the burner. What I mean by turning up the burner is, flirt with them all the time. Here is an example of what I mean. I have what I call my heat day. I would do it about a couple times a week. From the time I got up in the morning, I would spend all day chasing my girlfriend around the house. She would play along, I would tell her she was in deep trouble tonight when I get her alone, and all day long I would reach out for her, and every time I got her cornered I would kiss her on the neck just below the ear, she loved that. I would spend time telling her all day about the things I was going to do to her tonight. I wouldn't hold back and talk really (I mean REALLY) nasty. She would get to the point of going into a room with other people in it to tease me, because she knew what happened if I got her alone in a room. Even when we would go into a room with other people I would look at her with my big blue eyes and she knew what was on my mind, and laugh. By the end of the day I would have her so hot, that she would drag me upstairs. Then I followed through with all those nasty threats I have been making all day. You have to let them know that they are the one that lights your fire. What would have been nicer if my girlfriend did the same for me on occasion. Granted she would respond to my heat day, but she wouldn't start one with me. I guess she figured that if I wasn't in heat for her that day I wasn't interested. That is far from the truth, I tried to talk to her about it. But she had already gotten to the point of looking for greener pastures. My father has a good theory I would like to share with you now; it is called the Want/Want Theory. My father says that to keep the heat alive in a marriage you have to take turns being the wanted and the wanter. When you can take turns being the wanter, as an example my heat day. Then some days being the wanted, playing hard to get, (a little).

Then that keeps the heat up in a relationship. It is when one person is always the wanted or the wanter that things start to fall apart. When you are always the wanted, the ego will tell you that they always want me so some of the appeal of it all will go. When you are always the wanter, you might feel after a while that you are barking up the wrong tree. And look for someone that will respond better to your barking. That is where it takes effort on both parts to keep the burner turned up. You can be with someone for a long time and still have heat. It takes work; you can make your relationship better. Sex is not love, but it is one of the most important parts of love. It is the raw feelings you have for each other.

All the kissing and hugging in the world needs the passion of hot sex to back it up. When you first meet your mate, the main drive is sex, after a time of being together the main drive for the relationship is the caring for each other and looking out for each other. But you need that hot sex to keep the heat alive. My girlfriend got sex anytime she wanted, but the only time I got sex, was when I wanted it. This was where things were wrong in our relationship. I became the Wanter all the time and when I tried to become the wanted she would accept it as me not interested. All the talking in the world couldn't change the way she felt about this. She has had too many past experiences where she most likely spent most of the time, being the wanter and not the wanted. Once she became the wanter again, it would remind her of the old days when she couldn't get any attention and it would throw her on the defense.

I would like to talk about other forms of affection other than sex.

Let's start off with kissing. When you first meet someone you don't just kiss them you kiss them like you want them in bed right now. After time of being together kissing may fall into a habit or you just kiss her good night or before you leave. This is where you can make a big difference. Now don't get me wrong there is nothing wrong with a quick kiss from time to time. But a couple times a day you should make that kiss more than just a quick peck. You should stop her from whatever she is doing and turn her around and lay a kiss on her that would stop a freight train. We all get in a hurry and if we kiss at all it is out of habit, not heat. Put some heat into that kiss, every so often. Let her know that kiss means, if we had the time I would drag you upstairs. If you put some of these kisses into your daily life then they will know that you are in love with them and the kisses are not just out of habit.

You should avoid not kissing your mate, we all get so caught up in the day to day living that sometimes, not kissing her or quick kisses don't really carry all that much meaning.

Holding and Hugging

This sometimes will mean more to a person than a kiss. I am most likely going to reveal my age on this statement but my favorite kind of evening is on the couch watching a movie with my baby in my arms. Not that I don't like going out and doing things with her, but just me and her time, where the kids are doing their own thing and I can soak up the all the attention from my baby. I don't just sit their and watch, I hold her in my arms, or she would lay with her head on my shoulder. I would do all I can to make sure she was comfortable and caress her kiss on her during the movie and maybe even a little sneaky foreplay. This is my idea of a perfect evening with the one I love so very much. On heat days, I really got nasty. But just having her in my arms gave me the warmest and loved feeling I have ever had in my life. It should have been the same for her, and for a while I am sure it was.

Everyone needs to be held and hugged a lot. We all spent the biggest part of our day with people that for one reason or another is pissed off at the world and gives us all these bad vibes. But a little time in the arms of someone that loves you can make a lot of those bad vibes go away. Remember, feelings and emotion have energy in them, when a person puts out the energy our bodies receive it. If that energy (Vibes) is bad our bodies will adsorb some of it and it will affect us. That is why when you go to work, and someone in the office is in a bad mood it will affect the mood of the whole office sometimes. But when you are in the arms of the one you love, your body will adsorb the good energy from this person and it will give you a good feeling all over. That is why when there are problems in your life like bills, sick children, or other things that affect all of us, this is the time you hold your mate a little tighter and longer. That way they know that they are not facing these problems alone and know that you are concerned as well. It is the love and affection for each other that will give the strength to deal with these things and go on to face the next challenge that life will have to offer.

The problems might be worse or easier the next time, but the love you have for your mate is the constant. Your mate has someone that is strong enough to face the problem with them, or just have a shoulder to cry on, or be man enough to cry on hers. That is a funny statement, isn't it? Be man enough to cry on your girlfriend's shoulder. That goes against everything we are taught to be as a man. As a man I am supposed to be the strong one, the Superman that can handle all problems, leap tall buildings in a single bound, stop speeding locomotives. Well, I got a news flash for all women, each one of us supermen, have a Clark Kent we are hiding. We are weak and clumsy and get hurt and need someone strong in our lives. Some women only want to see the Superman in us; they think that we can handle it all with our bulletproof bodies.

That is why a guy will be strong only until he can handle it no more, then they will go into the I don't give a shit attitude. The truth of the matter is, they do, but as men we are supposed to handle it, and we are not supposed to show our Clark Kent, so we act like we don't give a shit. Because Real Men, don't cry or show weakness. I don't know how many times I have heard a girl say, well I have to take care of this because he doesn't give a shit. The truth is that he is just as worried about this as you are, he just can't handle it and needs her to be the strong one this time. Understanding these facts may help you understand why we as men act the way we do sometimes. It is good to take turns dealing with things, because with two people together, one usually has strong points about them that the other does not, it is the times when you are strong about something and they are weak you can jump in and be the strong one. Because their will be times when you are weak and they will be the strong one. As an example of what I am talking about I will use my relationship with my ex-wife. She was good at dealing with bill collectors and all the people that hounded us for money. I was good at day-to-day stuff, dealing with problems around the house and sick kids and cuts and death of a loved one. Being Superman at the time I single-handedly faced all the bullets and they just bounced off and I laughed. (Talk about male ego run a muck (hehe...)

But, I didn't give a shit about bill collectors or dealing with any money problems we were having during the time we were together. The truth is I sat up at nights worried how I was going to make those payments and keep us fed.

I, just as a man, wasn't allowed to show that this was more than I could handle and needed her to be the strong one with this matter. I should have been man enough to let my Clark Kent show a little. OH well, that is the past and I have my future to change that.

Sorry about that tangent I went off on in the middle of talking about hugs and holding. You should see by now that I do that from time to time. But it is an important part about why all of us needs to be held and hugged as much as possible. Next I would like to talk about the theory of being too clingy. First of all can you be too clingy? The answer is yes. As much as I would like to say no, it is true you can be too clingy. I mean if I had it my way I would quit my job and spend the rest of my life in my baby's arms. But I am a hopeless romantic. You need to give your mate some breathing room. As I said before, everyone needs time to himself or herself. When I was with my girlfriend, I spent a good part of my evening with her talking and being with her, but I tried to give her some time to herself as well. You need to be able to let go once in a while for them to breathe. What I mean by that is if she wants a girl's night out, let her go. I did this with my girlfriend and she had her girlfriend take her to the house of the boyfriend she was seeing on the side. I know that now, and I still say you have to let them go out. When I get my new baby I am going to dread the day when she wants a night out with the girls. But I am going to let her go. Mind you I will be pacing the floor the first couple of times. But you have to trust the one you love, just because my girlfriend did this to me, it would be easy for me to put my next girlfriend under lock and key. But that is not right to them; I would lose her in the long run. The first time you forgot to lock the door they will run. I must admit it will take me some time to really trust my new girlfriend. But for a while I am going to act on blind faith that she will not do this to me. I can't make her stay faithful to me this is something she is going to have to want to do. I am going to have to have the faith that she will. It will be hard for me; I loved my girlfriend so very much. The two nights she said she was doing something else and spent the night with her new boyfriend, I stayed awake a good part of the night just missing her. You know the sad part about this is, she knew I would be awake and can't sleep when she is gone and went and did this anyway.

This shows at the end how much she really loved me. I have a very hard time dealing with this. The betrayal is bad enough, but knowing that I would be up most of the night because my baby isn't with me, and be out with someone else really hurts.

But now, all that is in the past. There isn't a single thing I could do now to change it. I must go on with my future and trust the new one I love all over again. This really turns into a problem with some couples. You are not only living with the insecurity of your mate, but you have to live with all the times you mate's trust in someone has been broken.

I will talk a little more about this later in my section of trusting your mate. Being too clingy can also apply to smothering your mate with affection, hanging on them all the time. Everyone needs some space to themselves. You can be effective a lot and not hang on them all the time. There is a line of too much. Unfortunately I can't tell you were that line is, because with different people the line is different. You will have to wing this one on your own. Really I only have one more thing to say about this subject and that is you have to watch closing yourself in too much with your mates. You should have friends that you visit and be with other than your mate. You have to do things together outside of the house with friends and family. You have to give them the space to do some things without you as well. Personally this is one of my weak areas, I get so wrapped up in the person I am with that I tend to lose contact with my friends and family. Thinking that because she works and I work, all the extra time I have should be spent with my baby. I was wrong. I will have to find a happy medium with this, or I will lose my girlfriend by smothering her and lose my friends by not seeing them. But, as I said before that was the past, now I have the future to change that. Me being aware of it is the first step in change.

Chapter 13
Aging a Relationship:
The New Relationship High

In this chapter I am going to talk about the phases of a relationship and how to deal with it. This is what happens when you first meet your mate. Most of us can remember these feelings, of wanting to be with them all the time and all day long all you can think about is them. During this time the sex seems hotter, love seems stronger, and kisses are more passionate. Affection is more frequent. It is the time that starts the building blocks to fall in love. This is the section of the book where I am going to talk about why my girlfriend left me. My girlfriend loves this phase of a relationship. She thinks that this is what love is and always should be that way. She is mistaken; really this is what lust is. When you first meet someone I am sorry to tell you it is not love. Well, OK I will give it a little credit at this point, but not much. When you first meet someone you are mostly in heat for this person. It is only after the heat cools off a little that you start to really fall in love with a person. When I first met my girlfriend she said that she is going to love me forever, and really mean it. She wanted us to get married as soon as possible and spend the rest of our lives together. Telling me about how she had been searching for someone like me her whole life.

She wrote me love letters every day, telling me how much she loved me and can't wait until she was my wife. With the newness of the relationship, she had lust for me. This is only natural, but where the difference is she cannot make the transition from lust to love. She is thinking the feeling of lust (heat) at first is Real Love, when that fades she thinks that she is falling out of love and begins to look for someone else to have that heat with again. I found out after she left that she has done this same thing to other guys as well. Most likely, that is why she left the guy she was with to move in with me. The feelings of lust have started to slip and she started looking again.

I was told after she left me; within one week she was telling the new guy how much she loved him and wanted to marry him. He like me most likely is feeling that he finally found a girl that is ready to commit to him forever. He is wrong, I was wrong. She will have these feelings for him only for a while. Then she will go out and look for the heat she once had for him. I being the kind of person I am wrote this as my final letter to my girlfriend about 2 weeks after she moved out with him.

> *Dear XXXXX,*
> *I am writing you this letter for (his) sake. I am sure by now you are telling him how much you love him and want to be with him forever. You are even talking marriage. You are right now on the high of a new relationship. The sex is hotter, the feelings of love are stronger it is one of the nicest parts of a relationship. In a few short months, after the newness wears off you will start to feel he is not interested in you sexually anymore or you will lose the hots for him you have now. Just like what happened with you and me. This is when true love begins, you know I loved you now 100 times more than when we first met. See when I said, I love you more and more every day I meant it. We went from two people with the hots for each other to one person sharing our lives. When you tell (him) you want to spend the rest of your life with him, you really mean it. You meant it to me when you told me, I am sure. Just like you are telling yourself that I was not the one. Well a year from now you will have this same feeling for (him). This is where you find the forever love that you are looking for, after the hots are gone and he is the most important thing in your life. Why do you think I spent my time giving you*

attention, like I did? With back rubs every night and holding you, when you stop for a moment to let me.

I did this because you are the most important person in my life. My entire world revolved around you. That is why I made sure every day I was there on time to pick you up from work and spent my time with you in the kitchen just drinking coffee and listening about your day at work. I love that, it let me be a part of your life even when you were away from me. You know, toward the end when I was upset about you working late and all, I knew that you were seeing someone else that is why I acted the way I did. Even now, I am writing this letter for (his) sake, but mostly for yours you will never be happy with a person unless you understand what I am saying here.

Times got tough for us, but I am working it out with everyone, and keeping the house even without your income. Things would have been fine for us, but you didn't love me enough to try. The fact is that you say you love him now, and want to marry him.

Just a few short days after leaving me shows that you are this way. You know how much I love you, you lied to me, you cheated on me, you left me with no food or money and I still want to write you this letter so that maybe someday you can find the happiness you are looking for. Don't give up on him so easily. Remember only after the hots cool off will you find true love.

Love,
Martin

I wrote this letter with tears in my eyes. Some of you might be saying, God, Martin, you are such a sap. This girl cheated on you and lied to you and you still love her. My response to this is of course I do. Those were her actions and feelings; these are my actions and feelings.

I can't help the fact that I still love her, because when I said that I loved her forever I meant it. The fact that she cheated on me and lied to me will cause me to not to forgive her and never go back to her. But I still love her. A lot of us love people we really shouldn't. That is why you will find people that still love the mate that cheats on them, will stay with them. This is not healthy for the person, but they still love them. Their feelings and commitment have not changed only their mates have. If I let my heart become full of hate for this person, how am I not going to have the room in my heart for someone new to love. If I fill up my heart with hate for her when I meet someone new, I will not be able to commit my heart to this new person.

In time I can let go of the hurt, and the anger I have for this person. These are negative feelings, but the love I have for her I cannot let go of. She was so much a part of my life. You always carry something with you from the experiences you have in life. I need to carry the love with me, if I carry the anger, or the hurt I will not be able to love again for fear of the same thing happening again.

Then, you might be thinking, OK Martin I can buy that, but if you don't have the anger or hurt with you then what will protect yourself from getting hurt again. My response to that is nothing. See when I commit to the new person, I need to commit to them unconditionally. I have to be able to commit with my whole heart on the line. I can't put a condition of past hurt and anger into my heart. If I do I will hold back and not be able to offer the total love that I have for this new person. Now granted I will never be able to totally release the hurt and anger I have for my girlfriend. But I have thought out and faced these feelings. I will go more into dealing with the feeling in my section on dealing with a broken heart.

Anyway back to the subject at hand. Will my letter be enough to save my girlfriend from doing the same thing to this guy as she did to me? Most likely not, but we will see. Some of you might be asking, why do you even care? Well, because I have been in this guy's shoes. He is right now eating up all the attention and settling in for a long-term relationship that will last the rest of his life, little does he know that as the title of this section says, forever is six months long. My girlfriend talks a real good story, why, because she really believes it at the time. You can make yourself believe anything if you want to. When she told me she wanted to be with me forever she meant it. She was in the kind of relationship she wanted, newness, heat, and stronger feelings of love; she thinks that is what love is all about. But as I said in my letter to her it is only after the heat cools off do you really know if you love that person or not. This might bring up the question to you, Well Martin, if this is so, what about the statement of love at first sight? You know we really should change that statement to be more right. It is lust at first sight. It may seem like love, but it is not. Love comes later; love comes with spending time, to really get to know what that person is like and sharing feelings and yourself with them. That person must become the most important person in your life. In order for this to happen it takes time to really mean it. When you first meet someone this is the start of something special. It is the time when all of the love that follows it started. It is like building a house you have to lay a good foundation for the house to stand for a long time. Well, I have said, that a new relationship is mostly lust. Well I really don't want to not say that this is important. As the years go on this foundation must be strong to hold up to the bad weather that might occur during the life of the house. This is one of the reasons that truth in a relationship is so important during the first part of the relationship.

When you meet someone, from the very beginning you need to be honest and open to your mate. Otherwise you will have cracks in the foundation that the weather of time can break down. Starting a new relationship on less than the truth and not opening yourself up will cause the entire house to fall someday.

Another thing I would like to talk about in this section of the book is being you. Sometimes when we first meet someone we feel the need to impress them to get them to stay. We will act a different way than we normally do. We will do this during the lust phase of the relationship but as time goes on will revert back to the way we really are. In order for a long-term relationship to last you must be yourself from the beginning. If you meet someone and you are being yourself, and she is not interested then it wasn't mean to be. Because time will see through to the real you. If you are being yourself from the beginning then they know the whole package that they are buying. They know the weaknesses, the attitudes, and the feelings.

That is why opening up to them from the start is so important. The better this new person knows you, the better the chances are your relationship will last. Because if a person knows you inside and out and still wants to be with you then this could be the one.

When Lust Becomes Love

Well the next logical question is when does lust become love. This will vary from couple to couple. I just want to say that even though you are in lust at first, love does start to form from the very beginning. Just the foundation I talked about earlier. My father has a saying that if you haven't farted around them it is not love. Even though this statement is a bit crude, it is very wise and accurate. Love is a comfort zone. When you feel comfortable around this person and you show them warts and all then this is when lust becomes love. When the routine of everyday life starts to set in and the person you are with is a comfort to you after a long day of work. This is the phase when you start to feel comfortable with the person you are with, knowing that they are with you all the time. They have seen you when you are sad, angry, happy, and depressed. When they see you are sad, they know how to cheer you up. When they see you are angry, they know how to lend you an ear to dump on. When they see you happy, they are happy with you.

When they see you depressed, they know how to bring you out of it. A couple should be able to depend on each other for those types of things. Let's face it; life is sometimes full of crap. There are others in this world that want you to be just as miserable as they are. Your mate should be able to help you through this. You have the common feeling of love for each other to create some stability in your life. As an example I will use some of the things I said in my letter. My ex girlfriend is a CNA, that means she spends most of the day caring for sick and the elderly. It requires lots of lifting. Someday after work, her back was very sore; I would every night give her a deep muscle massage to help her with her soreness. On occasions the stress of business life would be a little too much for me and I would get stiff necks. She would take the time to massage my neck as well. One of my favorite things to have done to me is (no, not that !!!) a good back scratch.

Another important aspect of love is dependability. Every day as I mentioned in my letter I was on time to pick up my girlfriend from work. She could set her clock by me. If she would get out of work a little late or whatever I would wait in the car for her. I would greet her every night with a nice kiss and tell her how much I missed my baby all day. Lucky, or really unlucky at the time my business was doing poorly and I had the time to be there so my baby didn't have to walk home after a long day of work. You know what is kind of funny is the guy she left me for doesn't have a car, now she has to walk everywhere. I must admit this gives the anger in me some satisfaction. Well anyway, back to the point I am trying to make. When you get to the point where you are caring and can see your mate's needs on a daily basis then you are in the love stage of a relationship. This is a critical time of your relationship and demands the most work. It is almost a shame that the most focus of your affection comes at the lust phase of your relationship. When it is most important is the love stage. This is were it is easy to slip into taking the one you love for granted. You start not to appreciate all that they do for you. I think right now it is appropriate to spend some time on taking your mate for granted. Us men are the worst offenders of this action. We may have a mate that works, well not only will she work, but comes home to cook supper and do dishes and clean house and we are used to coming home to supper on the table and the house looking nice. This is something we will take for granted. I am guilty of it myself. My girlfriend would work all day come home and clean up the house and make me supper and she would have to mention to me, doesn't the house look nice.

I am a little better than most men, in that I would try to notice and say things about the appearance of the house. But not as often as I should have. I like most men will leave my clothes all around the house and not think twice about picking them up and when I had clean clothes to wear not think about the time my girlfriend spent doing laundry. Sorry, I am not perfect; after all even though I am wise to all that I have mentioned in this book, I am still a male. I did get to the point where I wasn't working much so I did some housework to help out. But when you stop and think about it, even when I was working I should have shared in the responsibility of the housework. I did help when it comes to making the mess. Some of this comes from my laziness, some comes from my ex-wife. With my ex-wife the kitchen was her domain. If you were in the kitchen at all you better have a reason and get what you need and get out. You know it wasn't till I was separated I found out that refrigerators were not self-cleaning. And even a self-cleaning oven requires some scrubbing. My kids did dishes for the first time in their life in my new apartment. They thought it was fun at first. I notice that I don't get away with that so easily anymore. Now monetary compensation is required, in order for them to do the dishes. Currently I am living with my oldest son. He is required to do the dishes and housework, because I am working so many hours at work and even on this book.

I work second shift and write in the morning. Granted I love writing, and as I am sitting here there are dirty dishes in the sink and dirty laundry in my bedroom. These that I took for granted being done by my girlfriend. It is a shame you have to lose the one you love to really appreciate all they do for you. That is were I can make a difference with my new girlfriend. I can help with the housework; I can appreciate home cooked meals. Right now I would give my left arm for a home cooked meal. Some of you might say, well then go out and cook you one. Well, call it the male in me I guess but cooking a home cooked meal then eating it is not the same. I can really understand why females will make a beautiful, full course meal and while I am pigging out, they are just picking at their dinner. Even a girl that likes to cook will get into a routine of making meals every night and dreading it. Now that I am single I hired my own Chef for most meals. Chef Boyardee will cook me any pasta dinner I decide to nuke in the microwave. I find myself eating out a lot, or every once in a while will take the time to make a home cooked meal myself. Of course while the kids are pigging out I am picking at my food.

You know I am thirty-six years old right now and until my girlfriend left me I had never done laundry myself. Even when I separated from my ex-wife I paid a friend of mines wife to do my laundry. Just think of all these years I have put on clean shirts, and pants and socks and not really appreciated the work it takes to make them that way. We as men take too much for granted. Every bit of affection I showed my girlfriend was not enough, to really appreciate all she has done for me. If you are a male and reading this, try this for an experiment if you are brave enough. Give your mate a week off, do all the cooking, take care of the kids, do all the housework, do all the laundry.

If you do this for a week and go to work every day as well, you will know what I mean when I say we as men take too much for granted.

Next I would like to talk about keeping the lust in your relationship. Once the love sets in we lose some of the lust (Heat) for our mates. As I said before this is only natural. To make a long-term relationship work you not only have to have the love, but you have to keep the lust in the new relationship. Heat is very important in a marriage. Keeping your mate sexually satisfied will keep them from looking for the greener pastures. Now I know what you are thinking, Martin, you are saying this and you are also saying that you did your part to keep your girlfriend sexually satisfied.

But that didn't keep her from jumping the fence to that greener pasture. Well, this is all true. See I did my best to make sure that she was happy and didn't look, but she had other ideas. See all the great sex in the world, most likely would not have kept my girlfriend with me. See I don't really want to brag, but I know a lot about feelings and girls, know where a lot of the "hot spots" are on girls.

I spend a lot of my sex on those "hot spots" which make me above average in sexual talent. It was her lack of lust for me that made her jump the fence. Let's face it; you can be very much in love with someone, and see someone else that you are physically attracted to. This is natural, if you truly are in love with your mate you can accept the physical attraction for just that physical attraction, and go on loving and being true to the one you love. Keeping the heat up with your mate will help them accept physical attraction for what it is. I know married couples that have sex about a couple times a week.

I even know couples that have sex once a week at a certain time the same night of the week. They have sex at this time whether they want it or not. This to me is sad; sex should not be a routine, and it should be spontaneous.

Now me, I am in the mood all the time. I could have sex every night, but not even that is good. It set a routine to it. You should skip a night or two to make it hotter when you finally do have sex. My favorite week is a girl's period week. I know, Martin are you nuts !!!! No, well OK a little crazy maybe. But let me tell you why this is my favorite week. I will spend all week, knowing that the person I love and want to have sex with I really can't have. This is fun, I will spend all week wanting her so bad and turning up her heat as well that by the end of the week, we don't just have sex, we have SEX. We would spend time count down the days till we could have each other. This is heat, not just love. Every couple will do this at first, the important point is do it every month. Make her so hot every month that she counts down the days with you.

Then make sure when you can, to back up all the talk with some stop a freight train sex. That is why I have my Heat days I was talking about in the previous chapter. Remember this statement, love comes from your heart; heat comes from your head. You can make or break a sexual relationship with your thoughts. My girlfriend was attracted to the person she is with, not because of love, but because of the heat she had for him. The only thing love had to do with it, was her lack of love for me. Even though heat seems stronger, love really is, if you have love with no heat then a person will stay, not be as happy but stay. If you have heat and no love then they will just transfer the heat to someone else. That is why it is so important to have the heat as well as the love. It will make them feel more complete, and be able to handle that greener pasture, and respect the fence.

Next in this chapter on aging a relationship I am going to talk about the importance of friendship with your mate. I touched on this in the previous chapter a little about talking but that is only part of it. I said this before but you should make your mate your best friend. You mate should be someone that you talk to about your feelings and life. This sharing of you is so important. I have found that a lot of couples have this problem. Do you know in my counseling of couples that in many cases I will know the person (inside) better than the their own mate does? When I advise them to talk to their mates more, they well say, but he/she doesn't listen. That is a big problem with most couples.

They may love each other very much, but not take the time to listen to them. Or when they do, go on the defensive about what their mate is saying.

You have to be able to listen to your mate without the defense on or a preset attitude about the subject being talked about. You will find in most marriages small problems, that whenever the mate tries to talk about it to the other mate, the other mate will have preset posture that they will take on the subject. This has a lot to do with the ego. In the first part of my book I talk about controlling the ego. It is true your ego will tell you that when this subject is brought up to act a certain way. This is wrong; you should face problems with your mate with an open mind. You should be willing to listen to them without preset attitudes on the subject matter. This is very hard to do. Your whole life you spend with past experience that will give you certain attitude about things. As an example I will use the night out with the girls. When my next girlfriend comes to me and says, Hey the girls want to go to a bar and have a few drinks, is it OK that I go along. My first reaction will be Not on your life. I will think that because my girlfriend used this to go see her new boyfriend. But thinking it through I will understand that my new girlfriend values her friendship with these girls and want to go out and spend some time with them. Then I will let her go with no conditions. I can't really say that I truly love her if I don't trust her to be faithful. Let me say this now, I don't regret the fact that I let my girlfriend go out with the girls I loved her and trusted her. I did the right thing at the time. She is the one that took my love and trust and betrayed it. My actions were good, the end result was bad. If I had it to do over I would let her go again, even knowing what I know now. The fact that I let her go is not why she went to see him. She would have found other ways to do that, no matter how tight of reins I keep on her. Where things went wrong was with her, she knew how much I loved and trusted her and took that love and trust and used it to see him. This is not love. Love is using the love and trust of your mate to have the freedom to spend some time with your girlfriends and enjoy yourself with no guilt. When you are spending a night out with friends and that is all that it is, you have nothing to feel guilty about. An exception to this would be if you don't spend time out with your mate, and spend all your time with your friends instead. You should have nights out with your best friend, and your best friend is your mate. If you are in a marriage or relationship and your mate is not one of your best friends, you need to try to change that.

They are the one you are sharing your life with, they should be the one you share your true feelings, ideas, and interests with. I would like to take a minute to talk about sharing interest with your mate. If you are a girl and your mate is a motor head. You can take some time to listen while he rambles on about this engine and car. You don't necessarily have to understand all that he is saying or be a motor head yourself. To enjoy his interest with him. If your mate is into Football, sit and watch a game with him. You don't need to understand all the plays, or penalties or rules, all you really need to know is what is his favorite to win and the score. You will do fine, don't ask him to explain everything, he is used to you not caring. And this might agitate him to have to explain it all, during the game. Remember false interest is easily detected. You don't necessarily have to enjoy the game, just be with him and share in the excitement that his favorite team is winning. Note—just hope that they are hehe…If you are a guy the same rule works. If your mate is into something, crafts, gardening or whatever, you don't need to become an expert in the field to share interest.

Whether or not you understand all the details of their interest is not important. The time together is. So when your girlfriend is out gardening, go out and talk to her about it. Grab a shovel and offer to help a little. Ask about her current project and let her ramble on about it and listen. This is all part of becoming friends with your mate. Most people have more than one interest, find common interests and share it with them. Remember you might even hate the interest, they have for something, but you do love them and it is important to them, so with very little effort you can share in their interest. Now don't get me wrong, you don't have to go out with her every time, or girls you don't have to start sitting through all of the games, just now and then will be good enough. Like I am into racing. If my new girlfriend would come out to the track with me on occasions and enjoy seeing the racing with me, that would be enough. Of course it is nice when you have the same interest in something, this makes things easier. But it is not necessary. If I find a girl that loves racing I am all set. If I find a girl that loves me but is not into racing, but will come to the track to spend time with me, that is great as well. There is only one more thing I have to say about all of this. If you're doing this to spend time with your mate and they don't really respond because they are so into it at the time, does not mean that they don't want you around. Just don't overdo it, spend some time with them then let them be on their own.

Bring them a coffee or Coke while they're busy with their projects. Spend your time talking to them about things and life at a different time. Just be with them. This action will start to build some of the friendship that you need. The best way to start this is start to talk to them about your feelings. Like I said in the previous chapter, find some time each day and just talk to your mate. If you do this without bitching at them about things at first, they might not tune you out. You know when I said not to bitch at them; I was not just talking about girls. Guys are just as bad about bitching about things as girls, sometimes worse. We are so used to using bitching to express our feelings that it is hard just to talk about them. You have to be able to talk about things without losing your temper about it. This will be hard because you are used to going on the attack to get some kind of response from your mate. The same is true about listening; sometimes you need not to argue about something but just sit and listen. If you have a different opinion on the subject, wait till they're all done voicing their opinion then you can tell (NOT YELL) your opinion on the subject. As I said in before several times the next is simple, but not easy. You have to talk out the differences in opinion to come to an agreement. Remember with every subject that you may argue about you have some parts of the disagreement that you agree about. Find those to use as the building blocks for the disagreement. (Did I lose you?) OK, we will use the old night out with the boys. Well let's start with the men's point of view.

Men's Point of View

1. I work hard all the time and deserve a night out with my friends.
2. I need some time to myself.
3. I am here with you all the time.

Women's Point of View

1. You never spend any time with me.
2. You never take me out.
3. I don't want you out flirting with other girls.

This is enough points for the purpose of the example. OK let's look at Men's point one. He goes out every day and works then comes straight home to his family. So point two and three seem important to him. Her point of view is that he never spends time with her. Yes, it is true he comes home every night to his family but when he gets home he is so exhausted he really just wants to kick back and not be bothered. She is feeling a lack of attention, which brings up her point two. And the insecurity of the lack of attention brings up point three. Now there are valid points in both sides of the argument. We will assume that if a guy is a faithful husband that really works hard, he really deserves a night out once in a while. While the women would even agree that statement she needs some real attention from him herself. The answer to this whole problem is quality time. If he would spend some quality time with her, she wouldn't even have her points of the argument. If he came home from work and devoted some of his evening to his mate, then she wouldn't feel like she feels. Also, it sounds like he needs to hire a babysitter once a month and take her out for dinner and an evening alone with her. If he did that she would feel like she gets the attention she needs and wouldn't mind him going out with the boys.

Yes, this is a simple problem and the answer is simple, but does require some effort. Most problems between you and your mate are simple ones. They just build to complex points in the argument. You will find that with talking to your mate and spending some quality time with them a lot of the issues your mate has with you will be talked about and something can be done about them.

Next in this chapter I would like to talk about something just as important as keeping the lust in a relationship and that is doing the little things. This is so important for them. They are doing things for you every day. Laundry, house cleaning, and all the other things that us males take for granted. Every day of your life together you should take some time and do something for her. It doesn't have to require money or a lot of time. The simple little things will mean more anywhere.

Some of the things that I am talking about are really giving her some attention. When she walks by flirt with her. Kiss her more often, hug her more often. When you are out together hold her hand. Talk to her more often, these all don't cost you a dime and are the most important. Some other thing to think about is when you go to a convenience store instead of buying a lottery ticket, buy her a rose instead. It will bring you better luck. When you are out shopping, and you see a cute teddy bear, pick it up for her.

Teddy Bears are one of my favorite ways of showing affection. Even though my girlfriend was with me only a few short months, she took with her a bed headboard full of stuffed animals. I would buy them every time I saw one that I wanted her to have, and I had the extra money. Remember this it is not the price of a present that counts it is the thought. So start thinking of her more often and pick her up things. Another thing I suggest is on occasion, put in some slow romantic songs in the CD and dance with her in the middle of the living room. Simple little things like this will help keep the romance alive in your marriage. Just make sure you back up all the romance with great sex. All the romance in the world will not make up for only having sex once a week or so. These things are so very important, because she is spending her time doing so much for you and you are just taking it for granted. All of us men are guilty of this. Another thing that can help is a night out with just her. Once you get into a relationship you will find that if you go out to eat, it is a quick meal, with the kids with you and that is all it is. Every so often you need to hire a babysitter take her some place that you don't normally go to, some place romantic with candles on the table and spend the meal putting aside all the problems and disagreements just give her love and attention. After the dinner take her out to a movie, or dancing at a bar. Just make sure you spend the whole evening giving her 100 % of your attention. These nights will help her see that she is not being taken for granted and that you do love her very much. I suggest having one of these evening once a month or so. Just remember after this great evening take her home and make love to her.

Next I would like to talk about something that will be hard for you at first but it does get easier. This is writing love letters. Love letters to your mate is very important. I can hear you men now, If I am with her all the time and I am telling her I love her and talking to her about my feelings, then why would I need to write her love letters, when I can just tell her. My answer to this is that sometimes talk is cheap, it is all too easy to rattle off an I love you. Not that we don't mean it but it is taking the time to put something in writing will show her that you really do love her and make her feel special. When you write them, put them in places where she will find them, while she is working on keeping your house clean, or doing something for you. As an example I used to put mine in the coffee can. That way when she would go and make us a pot of coffee she would find it. She loved those letters. She would be busy with housework but take the time to read them.

Now being a writer it is easy for me to write these, putting down my feelings and thoughts come natural for me. It will not be so easy for you to do this. But like anything the more times you do it the better you will get at it. Well, I can hear you now, Martin what do I say. OK I will help you write your first one. Here is something you can use.

Dear Baby (Pet Name)

I wanted to take a minute and tell you just how much I love you. You are with me every day and love me and

I know I don't show it as much as I should. I would like to ask you out on a date for this Friday. We could go to (Romantic Eating Place) and have dinner then go see a movie. Just think, you and me in a dark theater alone. After the movie, if you are willing I thought we could come home and sneak upstairs and I will show you just how much I REALLY appreciate everything you do for me. Let me know if you will be available Friday.

Love Forever,
Your Hubby

Trust me when she reads this, the juices will start to flow. In these letters you can be funny, talk nasty, tell her how much you care about her. Use it all. If you do this on a regular basis you will see a big difference in your mate and the love that you share. If you do the things in this chapter it will make a big difference in your relationship.

Chapter 14
Trust in a Relationship

In this chapter of the book I am going to talk about trusting your mate. I would like to say this statement. In a relationship trust is something that must be earned. Now saying that I will have to contradict myself by saying at first you must give trust to your mate. See when you first meet someone you have nothing to base trust on. This is where a leap of faith will have to occur. You will have to put you heart on the line and take a chance that it will be broken. This will not be easy to do. All of us have experienced a broken heart from time to time. We cannot let this past experience to determine whether the trust we give will be honored or not. I will go into that more later in the chapter. I want you to think of trust like this; it is a gift you give someone at first. If they really love you they will cherish and honor this gift. If they don't then, they are not mean to have it. Unfortunately, the only way to find out whether they will honor it is to totally give it. When it comes to trust there is very little gray area. You either do or you don't. If you think your mate is cheating on you, that is not gray it is not trusting. It will show in your actions to them and response to them when they want to do something that doesn't involve you. If they see that you trust them totally, it will show that you are a secure person. You might say, Martin you have talked about in this book, you gave your total trust to her and she betrayed it, how can you say, to trust someone. Well, I searched my own feelings for a long time to answer this question. You have to. If I don't then I will put my next girlfriend through hell, because of what she did to me. Chances are I would be not able to keep a girlfriend if I did not. Here is what I mean, I meet a new girlfriend and tell her how much she means to me, and how much I care for her, but when it came down to trusting her I couldn't then the rest really doesn't mean much. If I love her and care about her but am not willing to let her out of my sight, then I will lose her. I have heard it said that if you want to have a faithful mate you must not give them the chance to be tempted. Well, unfortunately they will be tempted whether you have them under lock and key or not. It is them that have to want to be faithful. Let's face it; all of us come across moments when we could be strayed from the path. When I was with my girlfriend, I had lots of opportunities to cheat on her.

I am an outgoing person that is easy to talk to, so girls like talking to me, about their feelings and lives. This will put some of them very close to me. I didn't cheat on my girlfriend, because of lack of opportunity. I didn't cheat on her, because she was the one I loved and wouldn't even think about doing anything that would hurt her. You might ask, well, now that you know, she was cheating on you, don't you wish you had taken some of those opportunities. My response is no, I am glad I acted the way I did and didn't stray from the path. Because all I would have done is, cheapen myself.

Right now I can sleep at nights knowing that I was faithful and didn't betray the trust that was put into me. Does my girlfriend sleep at night knowing what she did to me?

Yes, most likely she does, she doesn't have the same value of love that I have. But by the same token she will never have the true love and trust that someday I will have. You know toward the end of our relationship I let her go out with her friends, because I trusted her. Eventually, I knew about the other guy and let her go because when it came down to it, it really didn't matter. What I mean by that is, I would let her go "out with the girls" even though I new she was going to see him. By then even a lock and key would not have prevented her from seeing him. As far as I was really concerned was that if she was not going to be faithful to me, then she might as well spend her time with him. Will she cheat on him? Yes most likely after the newness wears off and she goes and tries to find the heat again. You know what is kind of funny, when you think about it is, she ended up not really cheating on me, but cheating on him with me. What I mean by that is, she knowing that she was going with him for a month she would come home and had great sex with me. This act alone shows that she doesn't really love him. If she truly loves him, she should not have been having sex with me. You really should not be having sex with someone you don't love. Now I am not without sin in that department by any means. I have had sex with girls that I didn't really love, but that's all it was sex. But I wasn't involved with anyone else at the time that I betrayed to do this. That is the difference, if sex was just sex with her, then that explains some why she had sex with me that last night. But having sex with me and being in love with him is not right.

You might be saying to yourself, Martin if you are so insightful with women and spent time talking to your girlfriend then why didn't you know she was going to find someone else. See, she meets her boyfriend during a training session about a month before she left me for him. Because of her past of cheating she was able to put aside her guilt and when she was with me, not show the double life she was living. She was so used to lying in the past that she could lie to me and not think twice about seeing him. After she left me, she was able to brag to one of her family members how easy it was for her to see him. And how much time she spent with him during that month they were seeing each other. She commented that I never checked her paychecks to see how many hours she was working versus time she really was spending with him. I would drop her off to work and she would walk over to his house instead. This really hurt me, I gave her my total trust and now she is bragging about how easy I was to lie to. Yes, it is true, a girl like that will be able to take me for a ride every time. I think that when you are in love and it is the real thing you don't have to question the amount of hours your mate works. Or if she is at work or not when she tells you she is. Unfortunately I will fall victim to this kind of person every time. In the long run, the joke will be on her. She will meet someone else someday and her new boyfriend will be the one that will worry about her working and checking her paychecks. He will know what she is capable of doing and will have to live with that fear as long as he is with her. You know I wouldn't even see a girl that could brag about screwing over someone and getting away with it. He may think it is funny now but wait till he is the one that she is lying to.

Sorry I needed to vent a little, anyway she went from me being the only one she wanted to be with to wanting to be with him. All the talking, attention, loving wouldn't have changed her mind. She had set in her mind that the love was gone from us and she now loved him. Just the way she committed to me so fast as well. The same way she will commit to the next guy so fast. She has the ability to lock out her feelings about the one she is with and totally commit to the next. This commitment is so strong that she gave up the custody of her kids, because the new guy didn't want kids around. This kind of commitment is not healthy. She is doing all this for a guy she will most likely toss to the side in a year. If you had told me that this would happen when we first met I would have said you are out of your mind.

But it did happen and that is why she really needs professional help. Since she has left, she has not asked about me or wondered how I am doing and getting along without her. She really doesn't care. She is only concerned with the new relationship and the heat that is with it. I have not seen or heard from her in any way since the day she left. I am totally shocked by this kind of person. She went from me being the one she was going to spend the rest of her life with, to not thinking about me at all. This is totally amazing. But it does show what kind of a heart she has. I was sold, hook, line, and sinker on the total commitment to me from the very beginning. It pulled me into a false sense of security with her. As I am sure it is to him right now.

Anyway back to the subject at hand, I know that by now you might be thinking Martin are you trying to tell me that when you get a new girlfriend you are going to be able to trust them totally. I would like to say yes, but if I did I would lie about other things as well. I will have all the fears, no trust, hesitation with the new person. But I also will let them go. I might pace the floor until they come back the first couple of times, but if I don't trust them then I can't really say I love them. Love and trust go together. That is why it hurts so badly when your trust is betrayed.

As time in a relationship goes on you will be able to trust them not because you are giving it, but because they have earned it. They will have proven themselves in their actions and love to you. I am going to take some time and talk about the biggest factors in trusting your mate. This is factor is Security. Security is an ego controlled factor that will allow you not to trust you mate, even when they have given you no signs that they are betraying you. Your ego will have the full cooperation of your imagination to back up what to believe. It is like a protection device to keep you from getting hurt. You might think at first well this is good; it is protecting your heart from getting broken again. The problem with this is while it is protecting you, it is pushing your mate away from you. I have counseled countless girls that are totally faithful to their mates, who are convinced they are cheating on them. This is the other mate's insecurity letting them think that their mates are cheating. As I may have told you in this book, in counseling I never give advice. I just listen; the person that is going through the problem to me is the only one that can advise what to do about the problem.

But with this problem, I do some advising. First of all you need to understand that you are not being judged for you. Most likely you are being judged for the last time this guy was cheated on. He has not been able to let go of the fear and anger of being cheated on before. My advice to you is this, you need to start talking to them. Share with them the love you have for them and let them know without doubt they are the love of your life, and no one else can come between you. Once they know that and if they still act that way there will be very little else you will be able to do about it. After that time will have to heal their insecurity. Sometimes this will not happen and they will end up pushing you away from them. I know I wouldn't want to live with my mate accusing me of not being faithful when I was. Now I am going to tell you something that I don't want you to take to heart, because it is not always true, but unfortunately enough times it is. Someone that will accuse you of cheating on them has these thoughts because the Greener pasture is tempting them as well. This is not always the case but it is the case enough to consider it when you are being accused. Not that they are crossing the fence, but they might be tempted to. Working on this person's self-esteem will help.

Next I am going to tell you about working on a person's self-esteem. This is truly a double-edged sword. You need to spend time building up your mate's self-esteem. This will help with their self-confidence and make them a better mate for you. I have seen all the time a mate treat the other mate with no respect thinking this will make them stay with them. When you put down your mate and keep them down you are not showing love for them. You are showing control over them. By building you mate's self-esteem it will make them a better person. They will take the time to care about their appearance. When I was with my girlfriend I always told her how pretty she was and how hot I was for her. She spent time every morning in the bathroom, working on herself and when she was done she looked very pretty. I happened to see her the other day ago and she looked like hell. She had let herself go really bad. Her new boyfriend must not take the time to tell her the things I did to get her to always look good. You know at the beginning of this section, I said this was a double-edged sword. What I mean by that is, sometimes you build up a mate's self-esteem so that for the first time in their life they have some.

They might take this new self-esteem to go to a greener pasture; this is the chance you will have to take. Building your mate's self-esteem is too important not to. It will give them security about your relationship and themselves. Did my actions of building my girlfriend's self-esteem get her to cross the fence? Not really, she had crossed the fence before, but I am sure that it made the fence a little easier to jump. Will I repeat my actions with my new girlfriend and build her self-esteem? My answer to that is of course I will. It goes back to the trust factor, I want to find a girl that will be faithful not because she doesn't think anyone else would be interested, but because she wants to be with me and only me. Something to keep in mind in building someone's self-esteem is that they may have never had any in their life. And this new self-awareness may change them a little. But this change will be for the good. It will make them a better person.

Next I am going to talk about another related factor: jealousy. Jealousy in a relationship is not healthy. It is caused by insecurity. I have seen a lot of cases where a guy or girl will put their mate through a living hell. They will have to explain every move they make and where they are every moment of their life. This is a real shame because most likely they are being judged for someone else's mistake. See right now knowing that my girlfriend was seeing her boyfriend for a month, and lying to me about working, it would be very easy for me to start to question my next girlfriend, every time I couldn't account for her whereabouts. This would not be fair to my next girlfriend. I just have to pray to God that I find someone that will love me enough to stay faithful. It is not a big thing to ask of someone you love. In today's world I have seen where a lot of people will cheat on their mate and lie to them. This is not the normal way of doing things. I have never really took a survey of how many do and don't. I don't think I really want to know. It will be higher than I think and this would really bring me down about relationships. See I am still in a hopeful mode that I will someday find someone true to me. I know of a few couples that being true to your mate is something they live by. If you are not living this way you are not doing right by the one you love.

You need to either stop or get out. I know what it is like to lose the feelings you once had for that person and find someone that the feelings of attraction and affection are strong with.

It is just a phase, if you leave the one you are with and go to the new one chances are in a couple of years you will feel the same way to that person as well. It is a never-ending cycle. This cycle can be reversed by putting romance into the relationship you have.

Chapter 15
Dealing with a Broken Heart

This is an appropriate time for me to write this chapter. As I am writing this part of the book, I am here doing this right now. It has been several months since she left me and I am still feeling the loneliness from her being gone. If you are reading this and have experienced this you will be able to relate. If you are currently going through it, you have my sincere sympathy. I want first to tell you, you are not better off. Everyone tells me that all the time. You would be better off having the person you love back with you and them loving you as much as you love them. But chances are that is not going to happen. So we must just go on. It is easy to see why a lot of suicides are committed during this time. I am not suicidal by nature but right now my life seems empty from time to time. I fill it the best way I can with friends and my kids and family. It is nice to have them, but it is not the same. When she first left me I completely stopped eating, I didn't eat anything for a week and a half. After that I got to eating about once every two to three days then finally I got to the point of eating every day. I lost forty-five pounds in three months. Luckily I needed to lose a little anyway. All these people that are looking for diet plans are really missing out. Just get your heart broke, that will do it. I am still going through the depression of losing her. In reading the first part of this book you will be shocked by that statement because I say it all the time in my book. Once you tell yourself you're in a good mood all the time you will be. Well the same is true about depression. I am allowing myself this depression. I worked hard for it and I plan to enjoy it !!!! Any time I wish to be depressed I allow myself to be. I know what you are thinking, Martin,

I think you have gone over the edge. No, not really, and here is why. After something like this happens to a person the worst thing you can do to yourself is to deny that it hasn't affected you. I am allowing myself this depression to help heal me. I have seen where people will hold it in and it eats at them until they become bitter and cold people or even commit suicide. By me allowing my depression I can think about the feelings I am having and why I feel that way.

I have looked for thousands of reason to blame myself for her leaving me. I came up with a few, but then I realized that they are not real. She left me because she really didn't love me. Could I have done more to make her love me more, maybe, but most likely not. I am a very affectionate and loving person. I spent every day letting my ex-girlfriend know that I loved her with all my heart. It wasn't enough. Right now beyond casual dating of female friends, I don't really date. I am still trying to heal and will not make a good mate to anyone until I do. I will be overly jealous, and insecure about our relationship until I do. When she first left me I cried every night that the girl I loved was in bed with someone else. I could not drop this thought from my mind; I still am bothered by it. Even after these several months, I get nights where I just lock myself in my house and spend all evening thinking about her and him.

This was supposed to be the person that loved me forever and me only. She is in love with someone else. I don't even see how that could be never mind trying to accept it as the truth. She has told her family that she is in love with him so much, well she told her family that about me not so long ago. I spent so many nights at home waiting for a knock on the door, and her telling me that she made a bad mistake and I am the one that she loves forever. After that didn't happen I started to accept the fact that she is convinced herself that she loves him and I am out of the picture. Living in a small town, I run across her and him from time to time. Only maybe about a half dozen times since she left me but enough that it really upsets me for a day or two after it happens. Not to mention all the people that think it is their job to tell me that they ran across her and him and how much they don't like him. Friends of hers love telling me about all the times they fight and how miserable she is being with him. According to them she is pissed off more about everything. Well, she can't be too miserable she is still with him.

In dealing with a broken heart you will have 3 phases that we all go through. These phases are as follows:

1. Hurt
2. Anger
3. Numbness

I would like to take a minute and talk about each of the phases.

Hurt

This is the first one you will have to face. When it first happened to me I was in shock at first, I couldn't believe that someone that I was so close to and loved so much was seeing someone else. I to this day, knowing everything that happened still only half ass believe it. I found out from others that she was seeing him for almost two months and living with me. This is a hard fact, but my ego can't swallow it. It is just more than my ego fighting this, it is my heart as well. She would come home and cuddle with me and make love to me after spending time with him. How someone can do this and be so convincing is beyond me. Hurt is the hardest of the feelings to deal with; you have a huge hole in your life. I spent so much time crying and wishing that all this were just a bad dream. Even now writing about all of this I can feel the hurt returning to me. I have gone through so much since she left, everything from locking myself in the house to not ever being here. Nothing seems to make a difference; the only thing that will cure me is the love of another. Until then I feel that I am going to have these good and bad days.

As time goes on, I am getting to the point that I am having more good days than bad, but once or twice a week I still have days were I can't stand it and get depressed. Even allowing my depression to happen you would think that by now I would be over her. Well, I am not, I have been listening to rock music all the time and hear songs that still stops me in my tracks and brings me down. I used to listen to country before I met her and when I was with her, I listened to country only. I will not even listen to country at all now. I am even to the point that if someone has country music on I will leave the room. This is some of the things that hurt will do to you. The same way with eating, I didn't eat, because the thought of food made me want to throw up. My eating habits are getting back to normal now. Hurt might affect you in different ways; in the depression you might over eat as well. It will affect different people different ways.

I want to take a minute to talk about this hurt. When you are going through it, it seems so overwhelming, do not let it get the best of you. It will pass, it seems like an eternity before it does but it does pass. You need to experience this; it is the first step in the healing. It is the foundation for the anger. While feeling this hurt be sure to focus not on the hurt, but the reason why you are hurt. This will help you in the healing. What I mean by that is like with me the fact that this was supposed to be forever and I was faithful and she wasn't is why I am hurt. Knowing these facts will help me in healing, because I now know why I am hurt and depressed and I can focus on those things and not just the fact that I am hurt. I know, I know, Martin you lost me. OK, having some fact to focus your hurt on gives you some of the unanswered question that runs through your mind during this time. Just focusing on the hurt itself, the picture is too big.

I have one more thing to say about this hurt, do not suppress it. Feel every bit you deserve to feel sorry for yourself for a while. The one you loved with all your heart has taken that love and betrayed it.

Anger

After hurt has run it course then Anger will set in. Anger is only a natural feeling that you will have after you are tired of feeling hurt and sorry for yourself. You come to a point were you can stop blaming yourself and put the blame on them, they are the one that betrayed you. When you are faithful and get betrayed, then you are the victim. As the victim you have to come to a point where you are going to want to balance the unfair way you have been treated. Anger is the most dangerous of the three phases. This is where all the hurt shows its ugly head. When I went through this phase I came up with at least ten thousand different ways to dispose of his body. Of course I really haven't got a mean bone in my body, so it was just thinking. During this phase, I didn't blame her for leaving me; I blamed him for taking her away from me. That is how much I loved her; I couldn't even accept the fact that it was her fault.

I wanted to believe that he had like a magical power over her and she was doing all this without knowing. It is amazing what your mind will come up with when you love someone so very much. During the hurt phase I was in disbelief that someone I was so close to and loved so much could do this to me. The anger phase brought to me the first clue; she did this and without a second thought about me or my love for her. To her it was like the light switch, she was able to click him and me off and on. It made me realize just how blissful ignorance is, during the time she was with me and seeing him. Granted I had an idea about him, but I really didn't know just how much she was seeing him and how she didn't care about my love. She could put on the act when she was with me and I bought it hook, line and sinker. GOD, I am getting pissed again just writing to you about it.

If you had to ask me what phase I am in now, well, see the problem with knowing the phases, it allows you to jump for one to another. I can jump into hurt, anger, and some numbness. I haven't really gotten to the state of numbness otherwise I wouldn't be able to feel the other two as strong as I do. I almost hate to tell you this, but better let you know now before it happens to you. While you are in the anger phase you will have the added bonus of feeling the hurt phase as well. Hurt and anger are together through most of the healing. You might ask OK, how do I tell which phase I am truly in. Well, whichever you feel the strongest at the time, at first hurt will feel the strongest usually. Then comes the anger, of course everyone is different you might feel the anger first, then the hurt. If you go this way you can bet that you will get to feel the anger again after the hurt. Most of us will get to feel both; I switch back and forth all the time. The hurt will feed the anger and the anger will feed the hurt. This is the longest phase of all I would like to take a moment and talk about something that might happen during this phase. A lot of people will find someone else, and start a new relationship. They do this in part to fill the gap that the missing person left and to get even with the person that left you. I mean it is very hard to deal with the fact that they have someone and you are all alone.

Entering into a relationship at this point is a dangerous thing to do. You will carry the anger into the next relationship and any pattern that is repeated by your new mate will strike an instant response with you.

Even as aware as I am about people and emotional phases and feeling, it would be hard for me to trust another for during the anger phase. I have dated a couple of girls since she has left, but not one of them has even gotten close to my heart. It is under tight lock and key right now. I have been badly hurt and every fiber in my body is protecting the wound. It is like having bad sunburn and standing in a room full of people, nobody and I repeat NOBODY is going to touch this sunburn. It is only after my sunburn is healed will I ever let anyone near me again. I am currently in a phase just these last couple of weeks in letting my heart open up a little. I started off with the easy stuff, like my dog and my kids. Yes, I said my kids, for a while even my kids were even out, don't get me wrong I still loved them, but nothing was getting to that hurt, not anything or no one.

Hopefully soon I will be able to open my heart to another mate. As the hurt leaves I hopefully will be able to replace it with love. I thought for a while my heart felt empty, it isn't it is full of hurt and anger.

Well back to the subject at hand, anger. There are many that never leave the anger stage. I have seen some that will not allow themselves into another relationship or give their heart to another; they become cold and bitter people. Part of this may be that they really don't deal with the anger, they try to suppress the anger and they do for a while, until it surfaces in other ways. It may surface with your relationship with your family and friends or in many different ways. One thing you can take to the bank is that some how or some way the hurt and anger will surface and make itself heard.

Numbness

This is the final phase you will go through. And it is not really a phase; it is what is left about your feelings after the hurt and anger have gone from you. Granted it will never go away 100% but you finally come to a stage were it isn't the driving force over your feelings about the one you have lost. I already know this phase from my ex-wife. I can be around her and have conversations with her, the anger and hurt is gone.

I have even been at bars where she would join us and some guy would put their arm around her or a stranger hit on her and it did not phase me. I know that someday she will have a boyfriend and that boyfriend and I might have to interact because of the kids, well, I am ready. I can feel comfortable with it, and not make an issue of things that really doesn't bother me anymore. That is numbness, will I have the same for my ex-girlfriend well I don't know, when my wife and I separated it was a mutual agreement. My ex-girlfriend left me in love and a hole in my life. It will take me time before it really wouldn't bother me to see her with someone else. I may never reach that state of numbness. What I am wanting is to reach a state that I am not missing being with her or feeling hurt because she left me. Am I there yet, you might ask?

NO, I have moments when it doesn't bother me as much as other moments, but all I have to do is see her or someone talk about her and I am right back in the thick of the hurt and anger. Currently while I am writing this my ex-girlfriend and that loser she is with (OOOPS their goes the anger again hehe…) moved out of the house they were in and have moved to another part of town. I don't know where and I don't want to know where. Trust me, I have many people that would love to tell me. Mostly people that know her but don't like him. By me not knowing I will not be avoiding her or looking for her when I am in that area. I know as small as this town is someday I will find out, but hopefully by then I will be far enough into numbness it will not affect me.

I want to take a minute and talk about the great stories of life and how it plays roles in the three phases. As you might recall, all of us play roles in our life in dealing with things that happen in our life. With my current awareness of life and emotions I play magician with most of the things that I come across in life but during this I played several different roles. First was a form of innocents, this is when she was with me and seeing him, I had a general idea she was seeing someone else by her actions but enjoying the innocence that I might be just overreacting to my insecurity over my unemployment.

After she left me and I found out about her having him, I was in martyr, for a long time. Martyr would relate to the hurt phase, well after Martyr came the Warrior, this would be the anger phase, and then the Magician would be the Numbness of course. Even with the knowledge of a Magician in almost everything I do, I am still not above the other roles as well. I will always be human and to play these roles just like everyone else. When something is familiar to me, meaning that I have experienced it before and am comfortable in dealing with it, I can play Magician. But running across a new experience I have to rely on the other roles to get me through it. The more time you can spend in Magician the more enlightened you are. My hopes with this book is not to fix your life, only you can do that but by being aware of what it is you are dealing with on a spiritual and emotional level will help you not to be so overwhelmed by the feelings and deal with the problem itself.

Understanding the roles of life and will help you get to state of numbness that you will need to go on with your life. See I don't understand why she threw away our relationship and left me, I most likely will never understand it. Not that this is wrong, she has her reasons I am sure. She is not wrong for leaving me; she made the right choice for her. Man, that was hard to say. But this is the reality of numbness that I am just now starting to see. Of course my ego says, how can leaving someone that loves you so much be right. But that is my ego talking not the way things really are. Someday I will need to forgive her for it. Only then will I be free from my own hurt and anger. Now don't get me wrong you can reach numbness without forgiving, but you will be haunted by hurt and anger. Only through forgiving her and yourself for losing her will you find the peace of numbness.

In the beginning of this chapter I talked about a statement that you will hear a lot if this same thing is happening to you. This is the "You're

Better Off" statement. At this stage of my healing, I hate that phrase. But I did notice that recently a friend of his wife and mine separated, because she fell for someone else, and what was my response "You're Better Off." I said it as an instinct for what to say, and then I choked after I heard that phrase come from my mouth. Unfortunately there is a lot of truth in this statement. If the one you love doesn't love you and leaves you are better off.

If they really loved you they would be with you. You know when you are going through all of this your mind really doesn't see the truth. It sees what you want you want it to see. I mean my girlfriend cheated on me then left me for him and I for the longest time refused to believe that she doesn't love me anymore.

I am still not totally convinced. We were so close, we shared our lives, our thoughts, our love for each other, and now she shares that with someone else. It is a very hard thing to accept. To me it is like I got run over by a car and I am staring under the front bumper saying this didn't really happen. I hurt; I see what is in front of me, and still not willing to accept it. This is part ego and part my heart. I wanted to write this section of the book, just in case like me you are tired of hearing this phrase. Your friends are telling you this because there is really nothing else they can say to help you through it. When they are telling you this they are right. If they don't love you then you are really better off without them you could be with them and them not love you, and cheat on you. That is something I am just now being able to see, once she left me I was better off than when she was with me and seeing him behind my back. The only way you would be truly better off is if the person you love loved you as much as you loved them. If you have this and don't appreciate it, then you need to think about things. I have seen so many people that have that and are still not happy.

In the next part of this chapter I am going to talk about healing yourself. In this section I am talking to you not only as a teacher but also as a student. What I mean by that is I have counseled hundreds of people on how to deal with their emotions during this time. I am talking to you in this chapter about it. Most of the people that I counsel, I know that I have really been helpful. You would think that with that kind of exposure to the same problem that I would be able to as they say HEAL THYSELF. Well, guess what I can't hehe…

See it is easy for me to help someone else, because all I have to do is have a sympathetic ear open to listen to him or her. They are the ones that have to deal with it. When I am counseling someone I do not offer advice. I can't advise a person how to deal with their lives. All I can do is to listen and repeat back what they say in a different light.

So they are not overcome with the problem. When I am helping someone I am up here on a hill, looking down at them in the middle of the trees. They see the trees I see the forest. But when it comes to my healing, and me all I can see is the trees. It is hard to put yourself up on the hill when you are so busy dealing with all those trees. Not to mention, the fact that even going through, it is hard to be at two places at once.

Anyway, back to the subject at hand. Healing yourself, I guess since I am not really an expert on this, I will have to give you some of the things that I do to help. First of all knowing what you have read so far in this chapter will make a lot of difference in understanding how you feel about things. By knowing the three phases you can then understand what you are feeling and not be as overwhelmed by it all. As I said earlier, just because you know this it will not make you immune to it. I got to experience it all, hurt, anger, and now even a little numbness. I got it live and in color with surround sound.

Here are a few things that I have done to help me through it.

1. Journal or diary—I designed a computer journal diary that I have talked about before in this book. It allows me every day to write my feelings about events that happen during the course of my day. Hand writing a diary will have the same effect. It allows you to talk to yourself so you can experience just how you feel about things.

2. Counting your blessings—This is where you look around in your life at your kids, family and friends and be thankful for the love and affection you do have in your life.

3. Learn to forgive them—You might say, Martin are you kidding, after all you have been through and how badly she hurt you, you're telling me that you are going to forgive her. Yes, someday when I reach

enough state of numbness. Why? Because it is for my best interest. As long as I have her to blame for leaving me hurt or blame her through anger then I will never really be able to heal.

4. Learn to forgive yourself—When someone leaves you through the hurt and anger phases we can all be hard on the person that left us, but you will find that you will also be hard on yourself. The "what if I had done this," questions and the "maybe I should have done this" statements. These are thoughts that will haunt you. You must be willing to forgive yourself for not acting on these thoughts. Because the what if's after the fact really don't matter. Whether they would have made a difference or not, chances are you will never know.

5. Give yourself time—Healing is a slow process, it takes time for hurt and anger to run its course. There is no set timetable or rules. The three phases is only an outline of what will happen to you. They may happen in any order they choose. Even, numbness may happen first, but it is a false feeling sense of numbness, then, you will later experience the hurt and anger. Some of you will get the pleasure like I did of experiencing the hurt and anger all at the same time. Talk about emotional battlefield. You will jump from one to another like turning the stations on a TV. You must get through this to heal.

6. Opening up your heart—This will be the tough one. You have to put aside your heart and anger to be able to open your heart up for your friends and family and possibly someone new. This is not something that may come easy. Your heart at this point is like a cut on your skin. You have this big old bandage over it. I know with me, it will take time to open my heart again. If you are not experiencing this through this state you are more adjusted then I am.

By keeping in mind these six areas you can work on, it will help you through the healing process. Maybe just maybe you like I am finding out that life does go on and it doesn't have to suck.

Chapter 16
Finding Mister/Miss Right

In this chapter I am going to write about finding the right person. I would like to start off with a little bit of bad news. There is no such thing as Mister/Miss Right. Sorry, this is a fact that we have to deal with. What you will find is the following.

1. Mr./Miss Not even Close
2. Mr./Miss No Way in Hell
3. Mr./Miss Yeah Right
4. Mr./Miss Possibility
5. Mr./Miss OK, Maybe with a Little Work
6. Mr./Miss Pretty Damn Close

In these categories you will find most are rated in the one through three zones. Some are in four and five. Every once in a while you will run across a six. When you meet the six, you better marry them, they are hard to find. I have had said to me in the past about some of the girls that I have dated that was not attractive. Well, that is because they were looking on the outside and not the inside. I have been with girls that are total knockouts and some that are a little overweight. All that isn't really important.

What is important is what is on the inside. Physical beauty will only make you happy at first. Here is some words of wisdom: It is better to have someone pretty on the inside than pretty on the outside. If you are very lucky you can get both. But it is not important. What is important is the beauty on the inside. It is a key element of happiness. A person with a kind heart is a person that will be able to make a better mate for you. They will not be self-centered and think of you instead of themselves all the time. I am sure that most of you that are single have met people that are really attractive, to find out that they are a dicks or bitches (gender considering). They are this way because they can have their pick of dates and are aware that they are wanted by many and are very conceited. (Note—I have lived with this problem myself for many years, hehe.) Really, I don't think I am ugly but I don't think I am a "Total Hunk" either. I really think that us average looking guys are the best to be with. I have seen rejection, hurt, and girls that are attracted to me. I know what is like to have a really good looking guy take a girl away from me. I even know through this last experience when a totally ugly guy takes a girl away from me. (OOPS, there goes that anger again.)

People that have lost someone for a better-looking person, get the awareness of rejection. They are not insensitive to do this to another person. Once you discover that looks really don't mean shit, in a relationship, hen you will be able to look for someone that is really compatible to you. Now, I will not totally commit to my statement that looks aren't important, because of the importance of physical attraction. You must have some in order for you to have a complete package. If you have someone that is kind on the inside and you are not at all attracted to them, it will make a difference.

One thing to keep in mind is that physical attraction is somewhat ego related.

Every guy wants a thin sexy girl on his arms. The kind of girl that makes other man stop in their tracks and wish they were them. The same is true for women, most want a kind of guy that other women would only dream of having. This is ego, run amuck!

If you are with someone that truly loves you, and that you are attracted to so what if by someone else's ego standard they are not what they want. If they make you happy that is what is important. Everyone has different standards of what they are attracted to. That is the nice part about all of this, no matter what there is always someone out there that will find you attractive. This is nice for ugly guys like me hehe...

Well let's take some time to narrow down what to look for in the right person.

First of all you must put aside your need for an arm piece. In my opinion a perfect way to meet someone would be on the phone. The reason I say that is when you are talking on the phone with them, you are interacting with the person and able to get to know them really well, then at the first meeting comes the prospective of physical attraction. That is when it really should be evaluated, after you get to know the person on the inside first. That is one of the reasons that we are hearing about Internet couples. People that get married after meeting on the Internet. They actually get to know each other on the inside first then they take that knowledge to the first meeting. If you can take the time to get to know someone you will do better in judging whether they are right for you or not. So many times we overlook a really good-hearted person because we are looking for that arm piece. I am not above this myself. Yes, my ego is alive and well thank you. I must give myself some credit; I do look for the inner person in most cases.

I have seen it too many times where both men and women will bitch that they can't find the right person for them, this is because they are not looking at the inside of a person. I have seen girls pass me by as well for that same reason. It is kind of funny really, they will pass me by and get attracted to some good-looking guy that treats her like shit, then come back to me to bitch about it. It seems it is great to have me around to talk to and a good shoulder to cry on when they are hurt, but when it comes to being with me for love they don't want to hurt our friendship. They have it in their minds that having a male friend that is always there for them is different than having a boyfriend. I have seen girls in tears telling me that they can't find a guy that they can just talk to and be supportive to them. Girls aren't the only ones guilty of this, most single guys that are out there in the "Open Market" have a girl on the side that they go to and talk about their problems. Not seeing that girl as a prospective mate because they are not quite what that guy considers attractive enough for them. To me this is sad, the kind of person that is there for you to talk to and a good shoulder to cry on, is the perfect person to be a mate for them. I can write about this because I am guilty of the same thing myself. I have seen girls that would most likely would have made me a good mate and not preceded it because I was worried about what my friends and family would think if I dated this girl. This was wrong on my part.

I am going to right now talk a little more about the importance of physical attraction. I have said earlier that this doesn't really mean shit. But in reality it does and we all know that. For most of us ego is a driving force in our lives. Even as much as my ego has been trained, I am still guided by it. It is why I act the way I do, it has set most of the parameters that I go by. If I am not physically attracted to a girl, I do have a stop button that will not allow that girl be considered for girlfriend material. Is this right, no not really but it is reality. Even if I let this girl become a girlfriend, and I am physically attracted to others, I would not be doing right by her. Now, don't get me wrong, you can have the girl that you have as a girlfriend, that is compatible with you and still be physically attracted to other girls.

That is only human, but if the one you are with, you are attracted to and you fall in love with them then, you will take the physical attraction toward another and know that you are really not interested because you love the one you are with. You have to learn that physical attraction is just that, physical attraction. It is not love, it is only one small part of love. You can have physical attraction without love, but you can't have love of a mate without some physical attraction. You can love a person without it. I mean I love my children and my father and mother. It is the combination of physical attraction and love that you will have for a mate.

Here is something I want you to consider. Physical attraction should not only include their physical looks. They need to be beautiful on the inside as well. A lot of men and women are pretty on the outside. What is the rarity is finding the ones that is pretty on the inside. Meaning, they have a good heart and are caring people. Too many times in looking for the arm piece, we will overlook the kind of mate that will be right for us. All I am really saying here is look a little deeper into a person. Look beyond physical attributes to the inner person as well.

I know what you are thinking, OK Martin you have made your point, but how do I really know who is Mr./Miss right? Well I will give you this questionnaire to help you determine. You need to use it when you are away from your boyfriend/girlfriend and have some time alone.

Finding Mr./Miss Right Questionnaire

1. Are you able to talk to them just like you would a close friend?
2. If this person weren't your lover, would they be one of your friends?
3. Does he/she miss you when you are apart?
4. When you are together do you have common things to talk about?
5. When you are together does he/she do little things to pamper you?
6. When you are together are you happy or sad most of the time?
7. When you are together how often do you disagree on things?
8. When you are away from each other if someone from the opposite sex approached you would they tempt you?
9. Does he/she satisfy you sexually?
10. Are you physically attached to this person?

Now let's take some time and look at each of the questions. Question 1: Are you able to talk to them just like you would a close friend? This is a very important question because I have seen, time and time again, girls that I have counseled that have me to talk to and a guy for a mate that they can't talk to. You need this friendship in a relationship in order to make it. I know lots of girls that I have been friends with for years, and have seen men in and out of their lives. They pick these men on the basis of physical attraction, whether they personally get along with this person or not. They are under the impression that their relationships are supposed to be love/hate and that is the kind of guy they seek out.

Question 2: If this person weren't your lover, would he be one of your friends? The answer to this question is a lot like question number

1. You need to have a mate that not only is your lover, but one of your best friends as well. It should be someone you can talk to and enjoy sharing everything with. If you have someone that you can share your secrets and feelings with then this is someone that will make a good mate for you.

Question 3: Does he or she miss you when you are apart? I put this as one of the questions because, when you find the right one, when you are away from them you feel like you miss them all the time. If you feel this way about someone, and they don't feel that way about you, then you're most likely in a one-way relationship. To explain this better, when I was with my ex-girlfriend she was living with me, but when I was working late or had to go out of town without her I couldn't wait till I returned to be with her again.

She was that way with me at first. She would write me letters and I would read them when I got home. Little things like that told me that she really loved me. Of course with her that love was subject to change. When you are away from someone, call them, write them, even if you are going to see them later that day. This lets them know that you are thinking about them when they are away from you. It is very important to them, this attachment and love.

Question 4: When you are together do you have common things to talk about? This question is important for long-term compatibility. I have mentioned early in this book that it is only natural that after a while the heat of a new relationship falls off a little. After that heat has died down, will you have common interest? When you meet the right person, you should be able to talk to them about your feelings and everything. It is not important if you share all interests, just some common ground interests so that you have something that you will be able to talk about in the future. One of these common interests can be just life. You could have a similar hobby, or others things of that nature.

Question 5: When you are together does he/she do little things to pamper you? As I have talked about in the previous chapters of this book, doing the little things are very important. They should put you before themselves and cater to you. You should cater to them as well. When you take care of them and they take care of you, this is what love is all about. Remember this is the most important person in your life you must cherish them.

Question 6: When you are together are you happy or sad most of the time? With this question you are going to have to look a little deeper into yourself. When you are with them you may seem to be happy on the surface but in fact you are not happy. Now I don't want to set you second-guessing yourself. So I will explain what I mean. When you are with this person, you may seem to be happy because of the sex factor.

But there is a lot more to the relationship than the sex. You must be able to determine, do you love this person or do you just love the sex. This is very important. I have seen some couples that will fight all day when they are together make up long enough for sex then go back to fighting.

Question 7: When you are together how often do you disagree on things? This is an important question because you have two different people acting as one. In a relationship you need to be able to agree on most subjects. You can't have too much agreement or too little. If you agree on everything one person in the relationship might be sacrificing their own opinions to satisfy the other. If you have to much disagreements it might cause problems down the road. What is wanted is a happy medium where each are allowed to voice their own opinions and the other to have respect for that opinion, even if they do not agree with it.

Question 8: When you are away from each other if someone from the opposite sex approached you would you be tempted by them? This is a funny question, because of our egos. You can see someone that you are physically attracted to, that is very human. When you find the one you love, you are able to accept the physical attraction for what it is. You are not tempted to act on your physical attraction, because you do not want to hurt or lose the one you are with. In other words the love you have for your mate is more important to you than the feeling of the physical attraction.

Question 9: Does he/she satisfy you sexually? This is a very important question because sexual satisfaction will keep you from roaming. I have been with a lot of girls. Some are willing to do more than others. I am willing to do everything, to sexually satisfy the one I am with. Well almost everything, I would not do a three way to satisfy my mate. If this would be her requirement, I would tell her to find it somewhere else. There are plenty of volunteers, I am sure. I am not into that I am a one on one person at a time sort of guy. To satisfy me you would have to be willing to do some of the things that I am willing to do. Many years I have had unbalanced sex, meaning I would do things that would satisfy them only they were not willing to return the gesture.

Question 10: Are you physically attracted to this person because sexual satisfaction is very critical to a relationship? You have to have the heat in the relationship to make it work. Like I have said earlier in this book, it is easy to have the heat at first. It is the heat that comes with love that will keep you interested in the future. You've got to have it to keep you sexually attracted to your mate after the initial heat goes. If you are not sexually attracted to a person once the initial heat is gone you will need to find someone else to replace that hotness you had for the person you are with.

I would like to wrap up this chapter by saying, look for someone that will make you happy, even if they do not meet all the qualifications that you require.

Chapter 17
Going On with Life

I have named this chapter going on with life. I have written this book through many phases of my life. When I started it I was married and had three kids, and not really happy in life because of the way my wife and I got along. The last part of this book was written when I was going through the dating process and had the experience with that girl. I am married now and I am happy.

I have found someone that is for me. The Miss Damn close, as I put it earlier in my book. We are friends, lovers and husband and wife. The things that are in this book, work. I am happy and I love life, and still have great days. I still haven't really had a bad day yet. In this wisdom from my teaching in this book, I can take events from a day that are bad and not let it get to me all day 99% of the time. Granted I am still human. Every once in a while I will let my ego run amuck and have periods of depression and more. The difference is I am aware of it. I have the knowledge to let it happen and be comfortable with it. Part of the knowledge is letting yourself experience emotions without letting them control you. My hope is that this book will help you understand yourself better and be able to deal with life a little better. Once you can experience emotions without letting them control you. You are well on your way to a happier and healthier life.

Chapter 18
Programming a Perfect Marriage

In this section of the book I am going to talk to you about programming a perfect marriage. This book has seen me through many stages of my life. When I first began the book I was in a destructive marriage with three wonderful kids. I have written this book over a ten year period of my life. My separation for my wife and kids and through my experience with a girlfriend that left me and now in a marriage that is very good.

You might ask, Martin are you still having great days after all this time, my answer is yes, I still love each one of them. With my current job I am working as a computer programmer and a web designer for a small company. I am able to outperform others in the company because of my organization skills and my personal drive based on the principles in this book. If this book changes your life half as much as it has changed mine, you will be very happy. You will love life and enjoy the benefits of getting the most out of it. Anyway, back to the subject at hand.

One of the first things you might wonder is how I knew my wife was the one for me. Early in this book I talked about finding Miss Pretty Damn Close. I found one.

When finding my wife I knew from the time I met her she was the one. Now I know what your first question is? How did you know? Well it wasn't my eyes, or my male sex part, or even my ego that told me, it was my heart. At the time that I met my wife I was dating other women who just wanted causal relationships. With them it was fine. Once I met my wife, I stopped dating everyone else. She won me over with her kindness and her caring heart. We started with being friends for the first couple weeks and then I asked her out and she accepted. It is funny because she is older than me and I having kids she thought it would be OK to date me because I was safe, there is no way in the world she would get involved with a younger guy with kids. This soon changed. On our first date we went out to dinner then went to a park to swing. It touched her in a way that she had not felt in a long time. She had always said in her prayers, God if I find the right one for me show me a sign with lightning or something like that. The first time we made love, I drove her home in a really bad lightning storm. She jokes about that now.

As I am writing this we have been married almost two years. The feelings of what happened to me when my girlfriend left is a distant memory and the numbness of it has set in. In reading back through that section of the book, I can remember how devastated I was during it, but I am so glad it came. I could have been with someone that really didn't love me and now I am with someone that does. With the experience of my ex-wife I would have relived in my girlfriend. What I mean by that is that she really didn't love me because she cheated on me. I know my current wife will not cheat on me because she has the same appreciation for our love and our relationship that I do. To me cheating on her is not an option because I value our trust and love. I don't even want to cheat. Granted I am still human if a good looking girl walks by me I will look. But my heart and body only belong to her. Why because her heart and body belongs to me.

There isn't any girl that I might look at that would tempted me to do anything that would hurt the one I love. Now I know what you are thinking, Martin, you're full of crap.

Well no, I am not and this is why, temptation is always out there, you can either make a decision to be tempted by it or not. It is not an involuntary action. You have choices, yes I am tempted to look at pretty girls but doing anything other than looking would violate the trust we have in each other. I will on occasions, catch my wife looking at some hunk of a guy. This is OK, I know I am the one that she loves and the only one that could be with her. OK, you might be thinking, OK I can buy a little of what you are saying but if I put a naked young blonde willing to do anything in front of you, would you be tempted? I can say yes, I would be tempted to look. But I would not be tempted to do anything else. See my heart and my body belong to my wife and to share it with someone else would be a violation of everything I really believe in. It would break down the world of my marriage, the thing that is the guiding stability in my life. To me cheating is like holding your breath. You need oxygen to live and my marriage lives on love and trust. In my past experience I have seen what it is like to love someone and find out what it is like to be cheated on. Doing that to the most important person in my life is not even tempting.

I would like to talk about a program that is currently running on TV while I am writing this the name of the show is *Temptation Island*. For those of you who don't know what it is all about, they have set up couples to go to island and they separate the men from the women and each have sexy singles tempt them into cheating. This is reality TV at its best. The ratings for this show are very high. I watched one show to see what is going on. From what I have seen on previews and the talk, they have all cheated, big surprise. Some of you might ask, OK you are claiming to be a faithful person how would you do on the show. I would say, I would do great, because I wouldn't go there in the first place. Everyone avoids temptation every day, if you don't put yourself in an environment to cheat you won't. We are all human and to care about others and be tempted with others is a human response. The overwhelming exposure that this show creates would break down your belief of being faithful. I don't watch this show mostly because I don't want to see others hurting others. I avoid those kinds of shows and movies they remind me of the time when I was hurt and put in doubt about the love and trust I have with my wife. If you expose yourself long enough to an idea or environment you will adapt. You will justify your personal belief of why you are faithful and start allowing yourself the temptation.

The episode I watched was the second to the last one where they were going on the big dates. The biggest thing I noticed is that everyone

MARTIN WHITE

has something they say they are having with their dates is connectivity. You hear the men and women saying the same thing they pick the person they wanted their final date with because they have a connection with that person and feel at ease and are able to relate to the person they pick.

Little do they know they could have the same relationship with the one they are cheating on. Every one of us can. That is one of the keys to keeping a relationship alive. Earlier in this book I have talked about the heat that is created when a couple first meets. The excitement of a new relationship and every feeling that goes with that. A lot of people I know don't keep girlfriends/boyfriends because they get to a point in the relationship where they are feeling like they are bored with the relationship because it is not new and some of the heat has gone. So they find someone new and then break things off with the one they are dating. They do this only to repeat the pattern when they are feeling that way with the new person. I am not saying there is anything wrong with this, the problem is that this person in the long run will become lonelier. They will go from one relationship to another, not really caring about the person because they know that just around the corner is someone new. After a while of doing this they will not put the effort into making a relationship work. This will speed up the frequency of changeovers to where they will not really appreciate the people they are dating at the time.

In having relationship after relationship a sense of emptiness will arise from it.

They start to believe that they are looking for Miss/Mr. Right, which if they would run across someone that would be right for them, they will just become another tried and failed in the series. The funny part about this is even if they decide this is the one and the other is playing the series and don't feel that way, then it will end and they will justify themselves with I really tried. It takes two to end the pattern. To end this pattern you will have to forget your experiences in the past with the others and judge this person on their qualities and not how you compare them with past relationships. This will be hard to do. Your basic instinct will be to judge them by others you knew in the past. You will

174

have to keep in mind that they are different and need to be looked at in a different light.

OK sorry for the tangent, back to the subject at hand. The name of this section of the book is called programming a perfect marriage. Now being a computer programmer I am going to show you the program for a perfect marriage. For those of you who do not understand computer programming just read what each line says and follow the line reference numbers.

Here are some Basic programming commands so you will be able to follow the program.

CLS—Clear the screen.

LOCATE 3,25:—Means at screen location 3 down and 25 over put what follows.

REM—This is for Remarks in the program not seen on the screen.

GOTO—means go to this line

IF / Then—This means if condition is true then go to this line number.

Input—means to wait until the user types in a response.

```
REM ******************************************
REM *** PROGRAM FOR THE PERFECT MARRIAGE
30 REM *** WRITTEN IN BASIC, BY MARTIN WHITE
REM ******************************************
CLS
COLOR 6,0,0
LOCATE 3,25:?"PROGRAM FOR PERFECT MARRIAGE"
LOCATE 5,25:?"WRITTEN BY MARTIN WHITE"
LOCATE 7,25:?"D—DOING YOUR DAILIES"
LOCATE 8,25:?"A—HAVING AN ARGUMENT"
LOCATE 9,25:?"B—FEELING BORED WITH
RELATIONSHIP."
LOCATE 10,25:?"F—FEELING NON ROMANTIC."
LOCATE 11,25:?"Q—QUIT."
LOCATE 13,25:?"CHOICE—";INPUT CHOICE
```

```
IF CHOICE="D" THEN 100
IF CHOICE="A" THEN 200
IF CHOICE="B" THEN 300
IF CHOICE="F" THEN 400
IF CHOICE="Q" THEN 500
GOTO 50
REM ***** DOING THE DAILIES **********
CLS
LOCATE 3,25:?"PROGRAM FOR PERFECT MARRIAGE"
LOCATE 5,25:?"DOING THE DAILIES"
LOCATE 7,25:?"TELL THEM YOU LOVE THEM MANY
TIMES A DAY"
LOCATE 8,25:?"DO SOMETHING SPECIAL FOR
THEM."
LOCATE 9,25:?"LET HER KNOW YOU ARE HOT FOR
THEM."
LOCATE 10,25:?"TELL HER JUST HOW MUCH YOU
APPRECIATE THEM."
LOCATE 11,25:?"HOLD THEM."
LOCATE 12,25:?"HUG THEM."
LOCATE 13.25:?"KISS THEM AS OFTEN AS POSSIBLE."
LOCATE 14,25:?"LISTEN TO THEM AND TRUST
THEM."
LOCATE 16,25:?"DID YOU DO EVERYTHING ON LIST
(Y or N)—";INPUT ANSWER1
IF ANSWER1="Y" THEN 150
IF ANSWER1="N" THEN 120
GOTO 112
120 ***** NO YOU DIDN'T DO EVERYTHING ON LIST
*******
121 CLS
122 LOCATE 3,25:?"WARNING"
123 LOCATE 5,5:?"YOU NEED TO GET BETTER AND
DO THEM ALL OR TAKE THE CHANCE OF LOSING
THEM"
```

124 LOCATE 8,25 SAY "PRESS ENTER TO CONTINUE......":INPUT A

125 GOTO 40

150 REM ****** YOU DID EVERYTHING ON LIST **********

151 CLS

LOCATE 3,25:?"CONGRATULATIONS YOUR RELATIONSHIP IS DONG WELL."

LOCATE 5,25:?"PRESS ENTER TO CONTINUE...":INPUT A

GOTO 40

200 REM ***** HAVING AN ARGUMENT *******

201 CLS

202 LOCATE 3,25:?"LISTEN TO THE OTHER'S POINT OF VIEW."

203 LOCATE 4,25:?"STICK TO THE SUBJECT YOU ARE ARGUING ABOUT."

204 LOCATE 5,25:?"EXPLAIN YOUR FEELINGS ABOUT THE SUBJECT."

205 LOCATE 6,25:?"TAKE THE TIME TO SEE IT FROM THEIR POINT OF VIEW."

206 LOCATE 7,25:?"FIND A COMPROMISE IF POSSIBLE."

207 LOCATE 8,25:?"IF NO COMPROMISE, TAKE TURNS ON WHOSE WAY IT WILL GO."

208 LOCATE 8,25:?"BE NICE WHILE ARGUING, DON'T SHOOT BELOW THE BELT."

209 LOCATE 9,25:?"CONFIRM THAT THE OTHER HAS A VALID POINT OF VIEW AND WHY YOU DISAGREE WITH IT."

210 LOCATE 10,25:?"SEPARATE YOUR LOVE FOR THAT PERSON AND THE ANGER YOU FEEL FROM THE ARGUMENT."

211 LOCATE 11,25:?"TAKE A KISS AND HUG BREAK IN A LONG ARGUMENT, EVEN IF YOU ARE PISSED.

212 LOCATE 12,25:?"TELL THEM YOU LOVE THEM AFTER THE ARGUMENT IS OVER."
213 LOCATE 14,25:?"DID YOU DO EVERYTHING ON LIST (Y or N) -:INPUT ARGAN$
214 IF ARGAN$="Y" THEN 250
215 IF ARGAN$="N" THEN 275
216 GOTO 213
250 REM ********** GOOD ARGUMENT ***********
251 CLS
252 LOCATE 3,25:?"CONGRATULATIONS YOU HAD AN GOOD ARGUMENT."
253 LOCATE 4,25:?"BUT YOU CAME OUT OF IT WITH MORE UNDERSTANDING OF YOUR MATE AND LOVE."
254 LOCATE 6,25:?"PRESS ENTER TO CONTINUE......":INPUT A
255 GOTO 40
275 REM ********* BAD ARGUMENT *********
276 CLS
277 LOCATE 3,25:?"THIS IS NOT GOOD, YOU DIDN'T CONSIDER THE FEELINGS OF THE OTHER PERSON"
278 LOCATE 4,25:?"YOU LEFT THEM WITH NO RESPECT FOR THEMSELVES AND YOU."
279 LOCATE 6,25:?"REMEMBER WHETHER YOU WON OR LOST THE ARGUMENT, YOU HAVE STILL LOST."
280 LOCATE 5,25:?"YOU WILL HAVE TO TRY HARDER THE NEXT TIME.
281 LOCATE 7,25:?"DO YOU WISH TO CONTINUE (Y or N)—":INPUT B$
282 IF B$="Y" GOTO 40
283 IF B$="N" GOTO 500
284 GOTO 281
300 REM ********** FEELING BORED WITH THE RELATIONSHIP *****

```
310 CLS
312 LOCATE 3,25:?"TELL YOUR MATE THAT YOU
WANT A LITTLE EXCITEMENT."
313 LOCATE 4,25:?"SUGGEST SOMETHING THAT
WILL BRING SOME SPARK BACK.
314 LOCATE 5,25:?"REMIND THEM YOU ARE NOT
BORED WITH THEM ONLY THINGS THAT YOU ARE
DOING TOGETHER."
315 LOCATE 6,25:?"PLAN A ROMANTIC DINNER AND
HOT SEX AFTER."
316 LOCATE 7,25:?"BE MORE PASSIONATE WITH
YOUR MATE."
317 LOCATE 8,25:?"PLAN A GET-A-WAY FOR A DAY
OR WEEKEND."
318 LOCATE 9,25:?"DO SOMETHING YOU HAVE
NEVER DONE WITH YOUR MATE."
319 LOCATE 10,25:?"TURN UP THE HEAT SEXUALLY."
320 LOCATE 12,25:?"DID YOU TRY SOME OF THESE
THINGS (Y or N)—":INPUT C$
321 IF C$="Y" THEN 350
322 IF C$="N" THEN 375
323 GOTO 320
350 REM ***** GOOD RESPONSE BORED
RELATIONSHIP ******
351 CLS
352 LOCATE 3,25:?"CONGRATULATIONS, YOU HAVE
DONE WELL."
353 LOCATE 4,25:?"KEEP IN MIND THAT IT IS NOT
THE PERSON THAT IS BORING YOU IT IS THE
ACTIVITIES YOU DO TOGETHER."
354 LOCATE 5,25:?"ALSO, CHANCES ARE IF YOU ARE
BORED WITH THE RELATIONSHIP SO IS YOUR
MATE.
355 LOCATE 6,25:?"NOW BOTH OF YOU ARE A
LITTLE CLOSER EVEN IF YOU HAVE BEEN DRIFTING
APART A LITTLE."
```

356 LOCATE 8,25:?"PRESS ENTER TO CONTINUE......":INPUT C$

357 GOTO 40

375 REM **** BAD RESPONSE BORED RELATIONSHIP ********

376 CLS

377 LOCATE 3,25:?"THIS IS NOT GOOD, CHANCES ARE IF YOU ARE BORED WITH THE RELATIONSHIP"

378 LOCATE 4,25:?"SO IS YOUR MATE. ONCE YOU START DOWN THIS ROAD."

379 LOCATE 5,25:?"YOU WILL FIND YOU OR YOUR MATE, MAY GET WANDERING EYES."

380 LOCATE 6,25:?"YOU NEED TO FIND SOME EXCITEMENT IN YOUR RELATIONSHIP OR YOU WILL LOSE THEM."

381 LOCATE 8,25:?"PRESS ENTER TO CONTINUE......:INPUT D$

382 GOTO 40

400 REM ****** FEELING NON ROMANTIC ******

401 CLS

402 LOCATE 3,25:?"START PLAYING TEASE GAMES ALL DAY."

403 LOCATE 4,25:?"PLAN A NIGHT OUT."

404 LOCATE 5,25:?"TELL THEM JUST HOW MUCH THEY MEAN TO YOU."

405 LOCATE 6,25:?"TRY DIFFERENT THINGS IN THE BEDROOM."

406 LOCATE 7,25:?"TRY DIFFERENT PLACES TO HAVE SEX."

407 LOCATE 8,25:?"HUG THEM MORE OFTEN."

408 LOCATE 9,25:?"HOLD THEM MORE OFTEN."

409 LOCATE 10,25:?"KISS THEM MORE OFTEN."

410 LOCATE 11,25:?"HOLD THEIR HAND WHEN YOU ARE OUT."

411 LOCATE 13,25:?"DID YOU TRY SOME OF THESE

(Y or N)—":INPUT F$
412 IF F$="Y' THEN 450
413 IF F$="N" THEN 475
414 GOTO 411
450 REM ****** GOOD RESPONSE NON ROMANTIC ********
451 CLS
452 LOCATE 3,25:?"CONGRATULATIONS YOU ARE ON YOUR WAY TO REKINDLING ROMANCE IN YOUR RELATIONSHIP."
453 LOCATE 4,25:?"KEEP IN MIND THAT IT IS NOT THE BIG THINGS YOU DO FOR YOUR MATE THAT IS IMPORTANT."
454 LOCATE 5,25:?"IT IS THE EVERYDAY LITTLE THINGS THAT KEEPS ROMANCE ALIVE."
456 LOCATE 7,25:?"PRESS ENTER TO CONTINUE......":INPUT G$
457 GOTO 40
475 REM ****** BAD RESPONSE NON ROMANTIC ********
476 CLS
477 LOCATE 3,25:?"THIS IS NOT GOOD, IF YOU ARE FEELING A LACK OF ROMANCE IN YOUR RELATIONSHIP"
478 LOCATE 4,25:?"CHANCES ARE YOUR MATE IS FEELING IT TOO. "
479 LOCATE 5,25:?"THESE FEELINGS WILL START TO DRIFT YOU APART."
480 LOCATE 6,25:?"YOU WILL END UP FEELING DISTANT.
481 LOCATE 8,25:?"PRESS ENTER TO CONTINUE......:INPUT H$
482 GOTO 40
500 REM ****** QUIT THE PROGRAM *******
510 CLS

520 LOCATE 3,25:?"ARE YOU SURE YOU WISH TO QUIT (Y or N)—":INPUT QANS$
521 IF QANS$="N" THEN 40
522 IF QANS$="Y" THEN 550
523 GOTO 520
550 REM ****** QUITTING ARE YOU MARRIED QUESTION ********
551 CLS
552 LOCATE 3,25:?"ARE YOU MARRIED TO YOUR MATE—"INPUT MAR$
553 LOCATE 10,25:?"THIS IS A REMINDER OF WHAT WILL HAPPEN IF YOU QUIT THIS PROGRAM IN REAL LIFE."
554 LOCATE 12.25:?"PRESS ENTER TO CONTINUE………":INPUT Q$
555 IF MAR$="Y" THEN 600
556 IF MAR$="N" THEN 700
557 GOTO 552
600 ******* DIVORCE COURT ******
601 CLS
602 LOCATE 3,25:?"WELCOME TO DIVORCE COURT !!!!!!"
603 LOCATE 5,25:?"IN QUITTING THIS PROGRAM IN REAL LIFE YOU WILL FIND"
604 LOCATE 6,25:?"IN A MARRIAGE LIKE MOST OTHERS THAT END IN DIVORCE."
605 LOCATE 7,25:?"YOU WILL NEED TO KEEP THIS PROGRAM RUNNING TO KEEP THE LOVE AND TENDERNESS IN A MARRIAGE."
606 LOCATE 10,25:?"PRESS ENTER TO END……":INPUT E$
607 GOTO 1000
700 ****** SPLITSVILLE *******
701 CLS
702 LOCATE 3,25:?"WELCOME TO SPLITSVILLE !!!!!!!!!!"

703 LOCATE 5,25:?"IN QUITTING THIS PROGRAM IN REAL LIFE YOU WILL FIND"
704 LOCATE 6,25:?"IN A RELATIONSHIP LIKE MOST OTHERS THAT END IN SEPARATION."
705 LOCATE 7,25:?"YOU WILL NEED TO KEEP THIS PROGRAM RUNNING TO KEEP THE LOVE AND TENDERNESS IN A RELATIONSHIP."
706 LOCATE 10,25:?"PRESS ENTER TO END......":INPUT E$
707 GOTO 1000
1000 END

Now that I wrote the program I can take the rest of the book and explain it. I wish we were more like computers and can just execute this program and not have all the habits and memories of past failed relationships to dwell on. See with a computer once you execute this program that is the only thing it will do. To make a relationship work we need to stick to the ideas in this program and forget the patterns that made past relationships fail.

Doing Something Special for Your Mate
Every day I start the morning off with giving my wife coffee in bed. She will have two cups I bring to her before she even has to get out of bed. This little treatment makes her feel like a princess. This is only one thing I do to let her know how special she is to me. Also, another thing I will do is when we sit down to watch TV, I always give her the remote. We will decide together what to watch, but she gets to be in control. Other things that I do is when she doesn't have to work and can sleep in I will set up her coffee and write her a poem so when she wakes up she can just push down the button and read her poem. You might ask why I do all this. Well doing this is nothing compared to the work she does for me every day. Things like keep the house clean and cooking and laundry, things that I take for granted that is being done for me. What I do for her is nothing compared to what she does for me. With my busy lifestyle it is hard for me to help around the house. I try to do as

much as I can in housework, but it comes down to very little. I know she is doing the bulk of it. One of the biggest things I try to do that helps is to clean up after myself. I realize that my wife has enough to do without picking up after my personal messes as well. This is something my wife and I talk about all the time. She has taught me that she is very busy with keeping the house clean and all the other things she has to do. I agree with her in that she is my wife, not my personal maid. I can show respect for her by cleaning up after myself. I am not always as good at this as I should be. I get times where I am brain dead as she calls it and will leave things undone not really thinking about the fact that she has to do it if I don't. My wife being from New York City doesn't have any problems expressing her feelings when I do. Hehe…

She had been single for a long time before she met me and her son is grown so she was not used to cleaning up after someone else. I don't think she will even get used to it and shouldn't have to. She is not my maid, she is my wife. Being as busy as I am most of the time I will go into spells where I am not working on cleaning up after myself and do need to think more about it. Usually she will bring this to my attention hehe. I then work harder on cleaning up after myself. There are times when I see she is tired and I will get up and do things for her. If she is too tired to make dinner I will make it. After dinner I will always help with the dishes.

Another thing I try to do is to think about things I do to surprise her. I will have her coffee ready in the afternoon when I come home for lunch and she is not there. Just little things to let her know I am thinking about her. It is very little effort compared to the many things she does for me all week, like cleaning the house and laundry and the other thousands of things I take for granted. We are on a very tight budget at this point in my life and I can't really spoil her with gifts, so I try to make up for it in good deeds.

Sometimes actions talk louder than words, I can tell you a thousand times that I appreciate her and love her, but if I leave messes for her to clean up after me, that tells her that my words don't mean anything. They are just words, but if I do actions that show her that I am looking after her and trying to make her life easier this will really show it.

Basic Rules of Arguing:

1. STICK TO THE SUBJECT YOU ARE ARGUING ABOUT:

It is hard sometimes when you are in the middle of a heated argument to stick to the subject at hand. You will find that it is in a argument that all the built up resentment and feelings tend to show up. I have been in arguments that I don't even remember what we started arguing about by the time we are finished. This is a good thing in one way it allows you to express feelings that are building up inside you. The bad part about this is that you do not get any decision from this kind of an argument.

So when you are arguing on a subject it is very important to stick to the subject at hand.

You can vent other things at a different time. This will keep the argument to what you are trying to do. Take time another day to express other things that are building up inside you. The more emotion you can keep out of the argument the better. Just deal with the facts and the points of view.

I have an experiment for you, I am sure with all the lawyer shows on TV have seen court room battles. This is a good way to deal with an argument. (Note: I am not saying sue them hehe...) Plea, your points of view in an argument like a lawyer would to a judge. Non-emotional, related facts, give them a chance to plead their case and make clear your mind and together make a decision on the facts presented together. This will be fun and challenging. You can take time to prepare your case, and present it. Call it Marriage Court. See even arguing can be fun.

Chapter 19
Programming a Perfect Marriage:
Doing the Dailies

In this chapter I am going to talk about daily things you need to do to keep your relationship alive. A good marriage or relationship requires work every day. Earlier in this book I cover this subject a little but now we are going to get into what to do to keep a marriage good. Let's take time to talk about the things in the program that will make your marriage good.

Tell Them Many Times a Day You Love Them
This is a very important step to do. In the course of our busy lives, we all get caught up in doing the day to day things that are important, work, house work, shopping, paying bills and all the other thousands of things we are responsible for just to live our lives. Sometimes we get caught up in our busy lives so much we forget to remind the one that we love just how much we love them. I make it a point every time I talk to my wife on the phone or in person or going out to go to work to tell her I love her. I am better than average with this but still on occasions my wife will feel like I am not giving her the attention she needs. This is understandable, I work forty hours a week with the computer company. Come home and have web design work to work on for the computer company I work for, plus one night a week I drive down to see my boys, plus I have computer clients in the evening at least one or two nights a week. So during the week if I do get an evening at home I am usually on the computer catching up with personal work of my web site and email or any other project, like this book. The point is that I am not spending the time I need with my wife. Now I really can't slow down

the pace of my work because we really need the money so how I deal with this is I make my time with my wife quality time, where she is the focus of my time. I talk to her, and find out how she is doing and listen to her problems and happiness. To my fortune my wife can express herself when she is not feeling loved and appreciated. This helps a lot, I know when we are starting to drift apart and this sets a warning flag for me to spend more time with her. Some of you will not have this going for you, your mate will not tell you when they are feeling this way and it will build into an avalanche and by the time you take time to talk to them they are not ready to talk because they are used to not sharing with you their feelings. Earlier in this book I cover how to talk to your mate. This will be important for taking the time to spend with them. Do it more often; that way they will spend the time talking and growing close to you instead of using your time you spend with them complaining about what you don't do. If you have a busy schedule like I do you will have to plan time for your wife. This may sound cruel but if you don't you will never make time for her. I plan quality time with her, just like if I was booking a computer client. They pay for your time and get your undivided attention, well you need to do the same for your mate. Plan the time for them. Also you need to plan some time for yourself as well. If you spend all your time for your mate and work you will not feel whole and giving during your time for your mate. If you have a busy life like I do you will find yourself needing time for yourself. I spend my morning hours doing this. I get up most mornings at 5:30am, even on the weekends. This gives me from five to seven for myself each morning. I will spend this on my computer working on my web site, checking email, writing, or just playing Nascar on the computer. This is my time to myself to spend. My wife has her time to herself in the mornings, she reads her bible every morning and prays. This is how she likes to start her day. Starting the day with time for yourself is very important, it allows you to feel like a person. So when you are ready to spend time with your mate you will be able to give them the attention they need.

Let Them Know How HOT You Are for Them

This will help you as well as them. As a relationship progresses you will find that some of the heat you felt at the beginning of the relationship will cool off. This is not a sign that your love for them it going away it is just a sign that you are getting in a rut.

This is a natural part of a relationship that will start to separate you from your mate.

I have talked about this in detail in the earlier part of my book about keeping heat in a relationship. This is something that you will have to work on every day. Make it a point to play with them. If you are like me you're hot for your mate but get into the busy mode and don't show it well. I make a point every day to do everything I can to show her that she is the one I ache for. See by nature I am a "pervert," so it is easy for me to do this.

Here are some of the things I do during the course of a day.

1. Get in a couple of very romantic kisses.
2. Cop a feel whenever we are alone.
3. When she undresses in front of me take and minute to fantasize and stare at the body that I get.
4. Play grab ass all day.
5. Expose myself to her.
6. Talk dirty to her all the time.
7. Hold her when I can.

Hey, I told you I was a "pervert." These are things that I don't feel I have to do but want to do to her. She must know that I am hot for her and know that she is the one that gives me wood. Sorry, I don't mean to be so blunt but that is the way I feel about her and if I don't show it she will think that I am losing interest in her. This kind of bluntness is necessary for her to get the message. Heat is not something that can be taken for granted. If it is not shown in a direct way they will start to feel you don't have that heat for them.

Trying Different Things in the Bedroom

Excitement in the bedroom is what helps to keep a good relationship hot.

Trying new things will help keep things alive. The thing you will have to keep in mind is the comfort level of your mate. They may not be comfortable doing certain things. I would like to go on the record right now, adding excitement to the bedroom does not include, other people, only your mate. Having others involved leads down a road that is a dead end for your relationship. Now don't get me wrong, there are plenty of happy couples out there that have open relationships where they include others. If both of the people in the relationship are comfortable with it then that's OK. I know what you are thinking, Martin, all your talk about love, and trust, you're supporting this kind of relationships?

What I have to say is yes! The reason I say that is this, I personally don't believe in it, but support that if this kind of relationship works for a couple then more power to them.

Now, back to the subject at hand. I can make every guy in the world a better lover with two words:

Slow Down

There I fixed them, don't you girls feel better hehe…For us guys I will try to explain what all the girls that read this book are laughing about, is the fact us guy like hot and fast sex. Now, the girls don't like quickies, hot and fast, they just need to have the other as well. Don't worry, girls, I'm getting to the point.

OK, guys I have an experiment for you: Close your eyes and imagine your mate in bed and waiting for you to make love to them. You want to jump in and "get busy" but stop, look at that body, she is totally giving it to you. You need to take time to enjoy every inch of her, she is giving you everything not just certain parts. You need to take the time to start at the bottom, her toes and spend a little time working your way up to her neck, this is a temple and every inch needs to be touched and kissed and tasted, you are the one she has chosen to give herself to, you are a hungry humble person that has just been given a royal feast. Every taste, every inch of this meal must be savored like it is a once in a lifetime meal that when you are done you will never experience again. Everything from the appetizers to the main meal should be done slowly building intensity to the main meal. After it is over you return to the humble person that just received a gift from the Gods.

Guys, try this and you will see some of the best sex you have ever experience. By the way, three quarters of the girls that read this just got hot thinking about it. This is what most women want. For you guys that aren't into oral, touching and kissing will do. For the rest of us guys, don't hold back...

Girls, sorry to put you through that but someone had to say it. Hehe...

Another thing you might try is role playing. This is fun and exciting. You pick situations and creators to become before and during sex. An example would be the nurse and the patient. You are in a hospital and she is your nurse on the night shift. I think you can figure it out from there. Doing things like this will help the excitement level, remember to turn it around, you be the doctor and she be patient.

Another little thing that I would like to toss into the bedroom is talk. Talk to your mate in the bedroom about your feelings or desires. Make that bedroom your place to share everything inside and out. This will add a sense of romance and sharing.

Tell Them How Much You Appreciate Them

This is a very important step in a good relationship. After a while of being together you will start to take them for granted, this is only natural. It is a comfort zone that will develop. You must take the time to tell them just how special they are to you. This is mainly for the guys. We work all day, to pay the bills, and chances are she is working as well, then she comes home and has to do house work as well. They are truly pulling double duty. We must be able to show that their effort is appreciated. One of the best ways to show that without words is to help around the house. Let her know she is not taken for granted and that you are willing to help. This is where action speaks louder than words. Not that telling her is not necessary as well. Between my company and the extra work I do for the company I work for, I am very busy most evenings, but I try to take some time and help with the house work. Granted, I am not as good as I should be about it. This is where I could use some improvement. Telling them how much you appreciate them doesn't have to be done on a daily basis, maybe once a week will do, but showing them how much you appreciate them by cleaning up after yourself and other small things you can do around the house is a daily event. This comes under taking your mate for granted in the previous part of this book.

Showing Affection for Your Mate

This is a very important part of your relationship. Every day you need to hold her, hug her and kiss her as much as possible. The daily things that happen in life happen to both of you. It is very important that each day they know they are loved. This will help them become stronger people. I am out in the working world all day long, some days are tougher than others, but I know that waiting for me at the end of the day is someone who loves and appreciates me. I know that when I get home it will be to a home full of love. I know that because I am told every day that I am loved. I make sure that my wife knows that as well. Most days neither my wife nor myself can wait to get home. We know that we will have an evening together with the ones we love. Every chance I get, I show my wife affection, she must believe totally that she is in love. This will help with trust issues as well.

Listen to Them and Trust Them

Earlier in this book I have talked in great detail about trusting your mate.

This is a leap of faith that will have to be made on your part. It is very important to trust them to have a healthy relationship. My wife and I have both been screwed over in the past. We have a sense of reality about it. We both know what it was like to love and trust someone and become victims of unfounded trust. I hold her heart in my hands, I can either cherish it or break it. The fortunate part about this is she holds mine in her hands. Why I said that is, I would not cheat on her because even the thought of me being cheated on by someone I love, makes my heart very sad. The trust and love I have with my wife is the basis of my happiness I have right now. I for the first time in my life have a good healthy relationship and have learned an important lesson about taking people for granted and love for granted, I can love and appreciate at this period in life.

Chapter 20
How to Argue and Survive

Now I know what you might be thinking. Martin, this section is on how to program a perfect marriage, if you have a perfect marriage then you wouldn't fight. I would like to say "YES" you will. Arguing is part of a perfect marriage. You have to keep in mind this, yes you are married and are one with each other. But you are also an individual with your own ideas and plans. Each one of you has different ideas, strengths, and weaknesses, this together as a couple makes you stronger, only if one side is willing to let the other side voice their opinions. As an example I will use my wife and I. She is very tight with our money; I am very loose with it. We argue from time to time about the way money should be spent. I have made her a little looser with money and she has made me a little tighter with money. Together we do well. The following is rules to keep in mind when arguing that will help with your relationship:

Listen to the Other Point of View

When you are in the heat of an argument it is hard to keep an open mind about the other person's point of view. Before you start to explain your point of view to the other take turns to explain how you feel about the subject you are arguing about. Remember yelling is always an option, you can express yourself without yelling about it.

Every once in a while I will get to where I yell, to make a point of how upset I am about the subject. But it is not necessary, it is me letting off a little steam. Keep in mind that even though you are a couple you are two different people; each one of you has the right to feel the way you do about a subject. Take the time to listen to what they are saying.

Explain Your Feelings About the Subject

In an argument you are in the heat of the moment, you might say your opinion on the subject you are arguing about but not explain why you feel that way. This will be necessary because your mate feels strongly about it for their reasons. Take the time to express you feelings about the subject. Just a statement that you believe this way and you don't back it up with the why's, is not going to get you very far in an argument.

It is like saying this is the way I want it and the hell with you. Even if you don't mean to say that, it is the way it comes across. Explaining why you feel this way will help them to understand your point of view. Consider that your point of view when you are talking about it. Make sure that is truly the way you feel. Sometimes in the heat of the moment you will commit to an idea that is not really yours just to win the argument. Make sure that what you are expressing is important to you and it is the way you truly feel.

Take the Time to See It from Their Point of View

After or before you explain your point of view, allow your mate to explain their point of view. When you are listening to their point of view you will have to put your ego in check and put yourself in their place. This takes a lot of self-discipline, if you are in the heat of an argument and have set your opinion on the subject in stone, you will not be able to consider your mate's point of view. If you take the time to see their point of view you will be able to understand. Keep in mind that most likely nobody is wrong or right. You have one opinion about the subject and they have another opinion about the subject. After listening to their point of view and considering it as an option, you may say to yourself hey, this is not worth arguing about and reconfirm that their point of view is valid and concede. Winning or losing an argument is not really as important as you think. Coming out of an argument getting to know you mate better and know that they had an equal chance to express the way they feel about something is more important than the Winner/Loser.

There have been times while arguing with my wife, I have listened to her point of view and it totally changed mine. There are also times when my wife has listened to me and agreed with my point of view. There are also times were we don't agree. This is OK, not to agree. If you have both expressed your option and each has considered it, it is still OK to feel the way you do. You are an individual with a valid point of view. In this step both you and your mate have won the argument. If this happens and a decision must be made from the argument, I suggest you flip a coin.

Another thing you might do is to concede. Let your mate have this decision and you hold out for something you really believe in. Taking turns with decisions will show your mate that you love them, trust them, and feel that their opinion matters.

Confirm That the Other Has a Valid Point of View and Why You Disagree with It

If the subject of the argument is something that you believe in. Then after you listen to the other's point of view and have let yourself consider their valid points, talk about your point of view versus their point of view. Show the considerations of what will happen in both decisions. Tell them that this is important to you. (Note: If you are on the receiving end of the statement this is important to me, then, if it is not important to you, concede.) Understanding your mate's point of view is very important. There might be something in their point of view that is not in your point of view. I am sure once you can understand your mate's point of view, then together you can come to a decision or compromise together. If not one of you will have to concede.

Find a Compromise If Possible

When you and your mate are both committed to your own points of view, then it is better to find a compromise if possible. Take some of the ideas from both points of view and make a decision together based on the points of view if possible.

This is the best way to handle the argument if you can make a decision together based on each other's point of view. You will have to determine if this will be possible.

Most likely it will need to go one way or another. The goal with this is to find common ground in your points of view and make a common decision based on common ground. See together you might come up with a third option that would work for both you and your mate.

If No Compromise, Take Turns on Whose Way it Will Go

When no compromise is available then take turns on which way you will go with the decision. You can flip a coin or just take turns it doesn't matter. The most important factor is that once it has been decided which way it will go, that you support your mate's decision. If things go well, acknowledge that their way did work and it was a good choice. If things don't go well, then be sure not to use that to throw into their faces, even if you were right. Why because someday the decision will go your way and it might not go right. The important thing is to support your mate and learn from wrong decisions. You and your mate, will have a better understanding of each other. This is far more important than who was right and who was wrong.

Guidelines to an Argument:

Stick to the Subject of the Argument

This is one of the most important steps to having a good argument. You must try to stick to the subject you are arguing about. This is not easy when you are in the heat of an argument. Some of the worst fights my wife and I had was because it started with one subject and went to another and another. Nothing came out of the argument but just being pissed at each other. When you ask me what started the fight I couldn't even tell you. If I can't even tell you what the argument was about in the first place, it only stands to reason that problem did not get solved. When this is happening in an argument at the time it starts to happen, switch the subject back to the original subject. you can get back to the new subject later. If you can stick to the subject you will at least get that solved and something good will come out of the argument. Be sure to get back to the other issues brought up. Remember some of those issues will not really be important just said in the heat of the argument. But some will be important, because they are to a point of something building up inside them. You will have to approach each one like it is important. Then weed out what is not. This will take practice. It is OK, if you are not good at this at first. The important thing is that you try.

Be Nice and Don't Shoot Below the Belt

This will be one of the hardest things to do during an argument. In the heat of an argument it is hard sometimes to not to get emotionally driven by the argument and say things you really don't mean. The best way to prevent this is to separate your emotions from the argument itself. Look at the facts of the argument and just the facts.

When you get caught up in the emotions of an argument, it will have you saying things that might hurt your mate. Remember once something is said, it can not be taken back.

You can really hurt someone with the things you say. They will think that is the way you feel all the time only you are exposing it now because you are mad. Things that are said in the heat of an argument can haunt your mate. They will think that is the way you really feel about them. When all it was is a dumb comment that should not have been said in the middle of being upset about the fight.

Separate Your Love for That Person and the Anger You Feel from the Argument

This will be one of the hardest things you will have to learn. You are used to fighting the old fashion way when you will lose your temper and say things you really don't mean. A better way is to separate your love for your mate and the heat of the argument. This can be done with sticking to the subject at hand. Keep the argument limited to the subject you are upset about only. Many hard feelings can come out of an argument if you don't. You must understand that you can love someone and disagree with them from time to time. In a relationship you are as one person but you still have two people involved, meaning you have two different points of view. Together with those two points of view you have to come to one decision. Showing respect for your mate during an argument is the key to this. Always keep in mind that they

197

have the right to feel the way they feel about a subject just as much as you have the right to feel. Most of the time you will find valid point in both, coming to a compromise is the way to find the solution to an argument.

Take a Kiss and Hug Break in a Long Argument, Even If You Are Pissed

During the course of an argument I will take a time out and hug and kiss my wife. Sometimes she is not to acceptable to this. She is pissed about what we are arguing about. That is OK, I will still take the time to stop the argument and love on her for a moment. Now I know what you might be thinking. Martin, you are nuts if you think I want to hug and kiss a person when I am pissed at them. Well what I have to say is, you are not separating the argument from the person. You might be pissed about the argument and the way they feel about their point of view, but they have the right to feel that way. You can't expect two different people to feel the same way about a subject all the time. Taking a hug and kiss break from the argument will take out some of the anger you are feeling and show your mate that you do love them and respect them. This argument you are having is not important compared to the love you feel for this person. You must be willing to show your mate that you can disagree with them and love them all at the same time.

Tell Them You Love Them After the Argument Is Over

Once the argument is over then be sure to spend some time showing them that you love and respect the way they felt about a subject. Arguments in a relationship can take a toll on your closeness to that person. You can't let this happen, you must take the time to show them that you love them and tell them you love them during and after the fight. If you can do this you will become a better mate for the person you love. Hard feelings will not develop from a disagreement.

You will be able to fight and show the kind of respect the other person deserves.

Chapter 21
Feeling Bored with the Relationship

A lot of times when you are with someone for a while you might find yourself getting bored with the relationship. When two people first meet there is the excitement of the new relationship and all the feelings of heat. After a while, with the daily routine of life and being together will feel like you are getting bored with the relationship and that is when trouble starts. Many will get to a point when their feelings might be telling them that the heat is gone from the relationship. This may not be true but just seems that way because the daily grind of life is creeping into your relationship. It is at this time some actions are required to put the spark back into a relationship. Good relationships don't just happen; it takes a daily effort to make it happen. Some of the following things can be done to put the spark back into a relationship.

Tell Your Mate That You Want a Little Excitement

First of all you need to tell your mate how you are feeling. This will have to be done carefully not to scare your mate into thinking you are going to cheat on or leave them. Little do you know if you are feeling this way chances are so is your mate. By telling them how you feel you can work on solving this problem together.

Earlier in this book I have talked about many different things to do, to bring back some of the spark in a relationship. I really can't talk about it enough, it is that important but talking to your mate about the way you feel is the most important.

If you can tell your mate that you are feeling that you want more excitement back into your relationship and then work on this, you can put the spark back in place.

Suggest Something That Will Bring Some Spark Back

Once you have established the fact that you want to add excitement to your relationship with your mate you can then work on some of the steps to build it up. A big part of this is putting romance into every day. Make sure you show it every day.

Show your mate that you want them and ache for them all the time. This will help them feel like they are special. Suggest some different places or different role playing to keep the excitement up in the relationship. It is very important that you keep in mind that you can't just expect the spark to come back. It takes work every day. Flirt with your mate all day. This will lead up to a point to where you are wanting each other so bad you can't stand it. The sex will be better this way. As males we are usually in the mode for sex but don't let it show very well. By showing how hot we are for them it will increase your mate's confidence and appreciation.

Remind Them You Are Not Bored with Them, Only Things That You Are Doing Together

This is one of the most important things in this section of the book. You have to understand that it is not the person you are bored with it is the things you are doing together that you get bored with. You know, if you are in a boring relationship and you find someone new after a year or two you will find yourself getting bored again. If you want to make things work with your current mate all it requires is finding new interests that both of you can do together. My wife and I like going to rummage sales in the summer. It is something we do together. We may take a Saturday and go to about a dozen or more rummage sales, we don't buy much but every once in a while we will find some good bargains. The important part about it is that we are spending the time together. We will do things like day trips to places we have never been before. There are times when I will do something my wife wants to do but I really don't like it. I will do it because it interests her. By the same token she will do things that interest me. The important factor is not what we are doing but the time together. It is good to find something to do that interest both of you. My wife and I both enjoy golf as well. We will go golfing together.

Plan a Romantic Dinner and Hot Sex After

One of the ways to break into having a more exciting relationship is a romantic dinner at home. Take an ordinary dinner and bring out the good china, light candles, put on some romantic music and any little detail you can think of to change dinner that night into something special. During dinner remind your mate of just how much you love them and how special your time is with them. After dinner help with the cleanup and then spend the rest of the evening giving them special attention. Follow through that evening with hot sex. This will take an ordinary evening and turn it into something special.

Be More Passionate with Your Mate

I have talked about this several times in the book. Every day is what counts with your mate. Every day they need to be shown that you love them and that they are the one. Romance in a relationship only happens when you work at it every day. Having a spark in the beginning of a relationship will be there, it takes work every day to keep it there. Show them that you love them every chance you get, sneak in those extra kisses and hugs. It will remind them that they are the center of your life.

Plan a Getaway for a Day or Weekend

Another good way to put romance back into a relationship is to plan getaways. This is where you and your mate take a day and get away from the daily grind of your life. You spend the day doing something special together. A whole weekend is even better. Book a motel for the weekend out of town and go have some fun. A lot of us have fun with our mates each year on the weekly vacation. Well plan a vacation for the weekend. Time away from house work and the hundreds of interruptions that occur during a normal day or weekend. Spend this time to get to know your mate again. In life you get very busy it is easy to drift apart. You need these times to pull you back together. If finances say no, do the day trips and not the weekend. Have a picnic in the park, while you are there play on the swings, go for long walks and just enjoy the company of your mate.

Do Something You Have Never Done with Your Mate

I know I have covered this before but it is very important. Life gets so busy and it is easy to fall in habit patterns with your mate. Do something special together that you normally will not do. Go to the park, go to the zoo, or anything else you can think of that is different than you normally will do. Keep in mind it is not your mate you are losing interest in, it is the things you are doing together. So be different. Try things that the other might enjoy even if you don't totally enjoy it.

This act will help show the love you have for them and help heal some of the things that are done because life is so busy you don't have the time to spend with them like you should. Here is a little test for you, if on Wednesday someone asks you what did you do last weekend and you can't really remember, then most likely you are in a rut. Break those ruts with doing something different.

Turn Up the Heat Sexually

Without beating the subject to death, sex with your mate will become stale unless you do actions to make it more exciting. This is not a reflection on your mate. It would happen with anyone you are with. Heat in a sexual relationship is like a campfire, if not attended it will just sit and smolder until it is all burned out.

You must take the time to (if you will to excuse the metaphor) throw another log on the fire. This must happen every day. Life will keep trying to put out your fire because you are so caught up in life you forget to attend to the fire.

Feeling Non-romantic

I will spare you the deal lines of the program because they are covered in other areas of the section of the book. The main point is that nothing in a relationship changes unless you do action to make it change. If you follow some of the steps in the section of the book you will find yourself in a better relationship with the same person you are feeling NON-romantic with.

Summary of Section

Now that I have covered the points of the program you are fixed, hehe.

If we were all computers we would be able to run this program and have a perfect marriage but since we are unfortunate enough to be human it will take an effort on your part to make things in this section work. You might ask, Martin do you have a perfect marriage? I would have to say NO. I am not a computer. But by following the basic principles in this section I have a damn close to perfect marriage. In life you would have to marry yourself to have a perfect marriage.

In a marriage you have two different people with life experiences, two different views of life and two different personalities becoming one. Of course you are going to have non-perfection in the union. The key is the more consideration you have for the other, the more the union will merge.

Chapter 22
The Final Chapter

This book has seen me through ten years of my life. I started it in the middle of a failing marriage. To a marriage that is the kind I only dreamed about so long ago. My life has seen many changes, during this time I went from married and making good money to self employment. It also has seen me through losing everything and sleeping on my friend's couch. It is seen my heart break with a girlfriend leaving me. It has also seen me now, happier than I have ever been in my life, with my current wife. We have one of those marriages you only see on TV. I can't remember how many times I have been told those kind of marriage only live on TV. Well guess what they can happen out here in non-TV land. This happens because of my efforts I have talked about in this book. You might want to ask, Well Martin are you still living the life you talk about in this book. I can say yes, this message is part of my past and part of who I am. Following the principles in this book has made me happy. Next you might ask, are you rich and successful following the principles. I would have to say no. If you wanted to find a get rich book, Ooops you just bought the wrong book. If you follow the ideas in this book it might make you more successful and rich. It will make you a person that will have confidence in themselves to give you a winning edge in the business world.

The main reason for this book is to make you not rich, maybe successful, but definitely happy. Life is so short, we are born, we live, we die. In the life of the universe it happens in a flash of a second. For us it is our time to make a difference in our own lives and others. Every person in this world is affected by another. We all work for filling out own dream and destiny while others are trying to fulfill theirs. One little thing I do, to remind me of this fact is when I am sitting at a traffic light I stop to look at the people around me and think about the fact that you are living your life and have a destination to go to that day. You have the responsibilities of child and wife and you have close friends to enjoy your time with. In the car next to you is someone who has those same things going on in their lives that is not even remotely connected to your world. You are the center of your world while the other five cars waiting for the light, someone in the car that is the center of their worlds. The two worlds, share a single a traffic light for a total of a couple of minutes in the span of their entire life totally unaware that next to them is a center of another world. Each day we encounter people that during the course of their life, part of their world intertwines with yours and then you go home. This may happen for years if you are co-workers. They are living at the center of their worlds and you are living the center of yours. For eight hours a day every day these two centers work together for another person who is the center of his world.

You might also ask, Martin you talk about stress management in this book, how are you really doing it living a totally stress-free life. Well, let me tell you about it.

I am currently working in the computer services industries where things need to be done now and because it is done with computers needs to work perfect. Well, I have stress in my life every day, along with my responsibility with my employer, but I still have the computer consulting business on the side that takes up a couple evenings a week. I am also currently attending school, trying to get my computer skills up to date. The stress level I face each day would be enough to send anyone over the edge. I am able to handle this stress load because of what I have talked about in this book. Yes, sometimes the stress of my life gets to me. But because of the principles in this book I can see the signs when things are getting to be too much. I also know that I don't have to let it overwhelm me if I don't want it to. Every once in a while I allow it to overwhelm me. I know what you are thinking, Why in the world would you want the stress of you life to get to you?

Well, I got news for everyone, it will overwhelm me whether I want it to or not. If I try not to let this happen then I am not dealing with the way I truly feel about it. One thing you will have to watch for after reading this book is to allow things to get to you. Feel your sadness, feel your loneliness, feel your fear, and enjoy each one of these feelings.

I know once again everyone is most likely thinking I have totally lost it again. No really, if you don't allow yourself to feel these things they will eventually shut you down.

The fine line in dealing with your emotions, is control. I said in the very beginning of this book that there are two things that will affect you in life: the internal and the external. Part of having a strong internal control is allowing the out-of-control part of your emotions be felt.

What I mean by that if you are sad, feel it, embrace it. Because if you don't you will suppress it. And every emotion that is suppressed will come back two fold. Suppressed feelings will haunt you. Your happiness and every aspect of your life will be affected by your suppressed feelings. You will find yourself thinking things are going well and you are happy in the way your life is going but under all of that is the sadness just waiting for a time to surface and remind you that you are not as happy as you are letting on. If you would have allowed these feelings in the first place you could have felt and started to heal from those feelings. If we try to control and block all feelings we will not really be living life and feeling it. In having to learn this myself the hard way, I had to define a line of what I will allow myself to feel and what I will let go. We deal with this currently only we don't know this. When something is upsetting you it is because you are letting it. You can either let this happen on a conscious or subconscious level. Not that you control your subconscious, but by dealing with it on a conscious level you can help your subconscious level deal with things better. This is the place to control you will have to monitor for allowing and controlling your emotions.

In this book is some of the ways to help you enjoy life. Life is something to enjoy. You have so little time to do so. In a blink of an eye, you are born, you grow up and have a family of your own, and then the next day you are a grandparent. It happened in your entire life, but in the big picture it happens in a blink of an eye. Every moment needs to be enjoyed.

Be sure to visit our website www.livingthesimplelife.com

Printed in the United States
68619LVS00004B/81

9 781424 101672